D1135521

...return on or be...
...due books. Renewal may
, quoting date, author, title a...

ST. HELENS COMMUNITY LIBRARIES

3 8055 00796 9827

# *The*
# WAY OF THE HORSE

NEWTON LE WILLOWS
LIBRARY
TEL. 01744 677885/86/87

| ST. HELENS COLLEGE | |
| --- | --- |
| 636.1 | |
| 129214 | |
| July 11 | |
| LIBRARY | |

# *The* WAY OF THE HORSE

## HOW TO SEE THE WORLD THROUGH HIS EYES

—

### JANE KIDD

#### CONSULTING EDITOR

RINGPRESS

NEWTON LE WILLOWS
LIBRARY
TEL. 01744 677885/86/87

Copyright © 1998 Eaglemoss Publications Limited
All rights reserved. No part of this book may be reproduced or transmitted
in any form or by any means, electronic or mechanical, including photocopying,
recording, or by any information storage and retrieval system,
without permission in writing from the Publisher.

Ringpress Books Limited
PO Box 8, Lydney,
Gloucestershire, GL15 4YN,
United Kingdom

Telephone: 01594 845577
Fax: 01594 845599
e-mail: ringpress@petbookshop.com
Visit us online at www.petbookshop.com

Printed in Singapore

10 9 8 7 6 5 4 3 2 1

# CONTENTS

PART ONE

# THE HORSE'S
# BACKGROUND

# Evolution of the horse

In modern times, it is possible to get the type of pony you want by breeding and cross-breeding. But, long before man was aware of the horse, it was changing and developing: these changes – evolution – enabled the horse to survive.

## From fox to Thoroughbred

Seventy million years ago, the horse was only about the size of a fox. A vegetarian, it browsed the plants and low-growing shrubs of swampy prehistoric woodland. But, as the threat from meat-eating predators grew, and other animals fought for the limited space available, horses found greater safety roaming the plains. Here they had to adapt to the new environment – wide, open spaces and a diet of grass.

They developed greater physical strength and the ability to outrun their enemies. At the same time, their teeth evolved to graze more efficiently and so complete the horse's 'survival kit'.

## Growth chart

Thanks to a remarkably complete fossil record of the evolution of the horse, scientists can chart its gradual change into the ancestor of today's native breeds:

**Size:** The horse became larger and stronger.

**Legs and feet:** These became longer and there was a reduction in the number of toes, with only the middle one surviving. This last toe finally became the horse's hoof.

**Back:** The back straightened and became much less flexible.

**Teeth:** The incisor teeth became wider and some premolars developed into proper molars more suitable for grazing.

**Head:** The front of the skull and lower jaw became deeper to accommodate the increasing height of the cheek teeth.

**Brain:** The horse's brain gradually increased in size and became more complicated in its working.

## How the horse changed

The earliest horse (*hyracotherium*) lived in swampy woodland and was a small, fox-sized browser. It had long, slender legs designed for speed. It also had three toes on its back feet and four toes on the front!

As the world around it changed, this little creature slowly grew larger, faster and better equipped for grazing dry grasses. Gradual development led first to a sheep-like animal (*mesohippus*) – with only three toes on its front feet – and then to one about the size of a modern-day Shetland pony (*merychippus*).

From this time on, it is much easier to recognize the features of the modern horse. Further changes, including the development of a solid, single hoof, helped increase its speed and strength (*pliohippus*) and then completed the evolution into *equus* – the forerunner of today's horse.

**Hyracotherium**
(about 70–60 million years ago)
This early ancestor of today's horse was only the size of a fox.

**Mesohippus**
(about 35–25 million years ago)
With longer legs and neck, the 'horse' was now sheep-sized.

**Merychippus**
(about 25–10 million years ago)
By this stage the horse was pony-sized and grazed on open plains.

▲ **Przewalski's horse,** the only truly wild breed still surviving to the present day, is closely related to the ancestors of domestic horses.

◄ **The first domestic horses** probably looked very like the now-extinct Tarpan. Horses resembling the Tarpan still live semi-wild — these are in a Polish reserve.

**Pliohippus**
(about 7–2 million years ago)
This animal was adapted for faster movement.

**Equus**
(less than 2 million years ago)
The forerunner of today's horse looked like a native pony breed.

# The heritage of the pony

**HORSE OR PONY?**
Not every animal under 14.2 hands is a true pony. The tiny Falabella, for example, has horse features but in a pony size.

▼ **The Exmoor** is one of the oldest pony breeds. It is recognizable as a descendant of the Celtic pony by its head, which is broad, with short ears, bright eyes and wide nostrils.

The difference between a 'horse' and a 'pony' is the height. Traditionally, a pony is 14.2 hands high or under and a horse is anything over. However, nowadays in international competitions the dividing line is a fraction higher at 148cm. But the ancestors of today's horses and ponies were *all* pony-sized and it was selective breeding, carried out by man, that produced the larger animals.

## Celtic relatives

In western Europe the pony's most important ancestor was the Celtic pony, which is now extinct. Although lightly built, the Celtic pony was very strong for its size.

The ponies found today with short, broad faces, wide nostrils, small ears, and big, prominent eyes, are almost certainly descended from the original Celtic pony. The Exmoor and Icelandic breeds still look very like Celtic ponies and have probably changed little since they were first domesticated thousands of years ago. They are thought to be among the oldest existing pony breeds. Dartmoor ponies may also be direct descendants of the Celtic pony and Dales and Fells are close relatives.

The Welsh pony is another part-Celtic descendant, though it also has some Arab features, including a dished face – Welsh mares were bred with a Thoroughbred stallion early in the 19th century. Such cross-breeding of ponies produces an animal better suited for riding and Thoroughbred blood has been introduced into many breeds.

In Asia, where ponies are working animals, the dished face is common. It was inherited from local ancestors who were related to the Arab. New Forest ponies, too, often have dished faces because they were cross-bred with Arabs in the 18th century.

## *Small is beautiful*

The very small Shetland is also a descendant of the Celtic pony. It has adapted to life in the harsh environment of the Northern isles off the Scottish coast, where food is often scarce. After many generations all members of the population are small, but this is an advantage – the Shetland needs less food to survive and breed. Despite their size, Shetlands are strong and in the past were used as pit ponies.

▲ **Ponies** are very strong for their size. Despite their small frames, they are capable of carrying or pulling heavy loads.

◄ **New-born pony foals** have the same proportions they will have as adults.

◄ **The Shetland** is one of the smallest pony breeds in the world.

► **The addition of Thoroughbred blood** to many pony breeds has improved their riding qualities.

# The hot and cold-bloods

As herds of wild horses migrated to different parts of the world, they underwent changes to adapt to their new habitats. Variations in climate and food produced their own types of horse. The two extreme types were the cold-bloods and the hot-bloods, who had different appearances and temperaments. Modern-day breeds of horse have evolved from these and from cross-breeding.

## Cold-bloods

In the northern regions of the world, the climate produced lush pastures. The horses that lived there became heavy, strong and slow moving. To help them survive the freezing weather conditions in winter, nature equipped these horses with a thick skin and a layer of fat underneath it.

Most of the work and heavy draught horses of today fall into the category of cold-bloods. The biggest breed of cold-bloods (in fact the biggest breed in the world) is the British Shire. These horses can reach 17 or 18 hands high, and

▲ **The Ardennais** is a typical cold-blooded horse. Massive, powerful and tough, it can survive in the coldest and wettest weather.

►**Cold-blooded horses** adapted to life in the north. Today, they are strong but docile and make ideal workhorses.

weigh up to 1300kg (2900lbs) – the equivalent of 17 fully grown men!

## *Hot-bloods*

Hot-bloods developed quite differently from their northern relatives. In the south, where they lived, there were less extremes of climate. As a consequence, southern horses had thin coats to keep them cool and comfortable in the hottest of weather.

Food was in short supply, so the horses learned to survive from poor grazing. This also made them lighter, although they were still quite large. In their new habitat there were often few places for them to hide in times of trouble, so they became swift to escape their predators.

The Arab and Barb are well-known examples of the hot-bloods. The Arab is renowned for its courage, stamina and speed and has been much used for cross-breeding. The Barb has a reputation based on sure-footedness, strength and endurance.

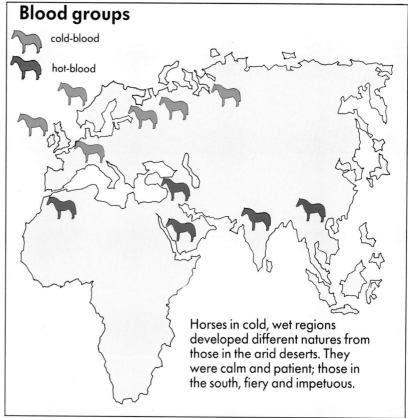

**Blood groups**

cold-blood

hot-blood

Horses in cold, wet regions developed different natures from those in the arid deserts. They were calm and patient; those in the south, fiery and impetuous.

▲ **The fine bone-structure** of the Tersky's head instantly betrays its hot-blooded origins.

► **Arab horses** have evolved to cope with harsh desert conditions and the constant threat of fatigue, hunger and thirst.

# The gene machine

The 'masterplan' of a foal's appearance and conformation comes from the genes he inherits from his parents. In domestic breeding, the choice of the right mare and stallion is, therefore, all-important.

## Passing on information

Inheriting particular looks or personality is all to do with 'genes'. Genes contain the information that makes every living thing the way it is – in a horse, they 'programme' whether it is, say, bay or dun; calm or high-spirited; athletic or clumsy. This information is passed on from one generation to the next.

Think of families you know. There are definite likenesses between sisters and brothers – they may all have a similar straight nose or blond hair. When you see their parents, you can tell where the resemblance comes from: they may have inherited features from their father and hair colour from their mother.

## Generation gap

Within that blond-haired family, however, there may be one who looks completely different and has, say, red hair. This is because some genes can 'skip' gener-

ations, and the red hair may have come originally from a grandparent.

The same goes for horses. A palomino stallion may be able to pass on his colour to his foals but, if he carries a chestnut gene from further back in his family, one or more of the foals could well be chestnut.

The information in genes also plays a part in programming characteristics of conformation and temperament. This can be used to 'plan' better foals. A long-backed mare and a short-backed stallion could produce a foal with the perfect length of back. But don't rely on two wrongs making a right: the foal could just as easily turn out with the same back fault as one of the parents.

## A bit of a gamble

You can never predict with absolute certainty what a foal will be like – breeding horses can be a real gamble. A foal can have pony-sized parents yet grow very tall, and grey parents may produce a dark chestnut foal.

But there are ways of lessening the gamble. High-quality stallions of known breeding are more likely to pass on their good points

to their foals. Combined with the best possible mares, the gamble becomes more likely to pay off.

## Combining breeds

There are many well-known breeds whose qualities are valued for cross-breeding all over the world.

The Arab is one of the most beautiful and ancient of breeds. They have been used for centuries to give elegance, endurance and spirit to top-class breeds.

The Thoroughbred, descended from the Arab, is a superb cross with practically any other type. Thoroughbreds add speed and agility.

Warm-bloods are very popular as all-round sports horses for dressage, eventing and show jumping. Warm-blood breeds such as the Hanoverian, the Dutch Warm-blood and the Trakehner are known as compound breeds – they are made by mixing Thoroughbreds and Arabs with local carriage horses.

Hardiness, cleverness and strength are all qualities found in the native pony breeds of Great Britain. They can make some very successful crosses – and many a Grand National winner has had a touch of pony blood.

►**Colour:** A foal may not necessarily take after its mother. It may inherit the colour of its coat from its father or even from a grandparent.

Some pure breeds can only be a specific colour but not so this New Forest mare and foal: they could have been anything except piebald or skewbald.

# Cross-breeding

| | Native | Draught (Draft) | Warm-blood | Thoroughbred | Arab |
|---|---|---|---|---|---|
| **Arab** | Can be a very good cross. High-quality riding ponies. | Too much difference in type to make the cross worthwhile. | A good cross with the lighter Warm-bloods such as the Trakehner. | Anglo-Arab. Excellent all-round show and riding horses. A very popular cross. |  Pure-bred Arab. |
| **Thoroughbred** | A successful cross combining the good qualities of the two breeds. The foundation for many successful riding club horses, show jumpers and hunters. | A popular cross which produces strong horses such as show jumpers and hunters. | All warm-blooded breeds make excellent crosses with Thoroughbreds. |  Pure-bred Thoroughbred. | |
| **Warm-blood** | Could produce a useful hunter or riding club horse. However, it could be a poor cross because Warm-bloods are themselves a mixture of breeds, developed over a long period of time. | Sometimes used to produce a very heavyweight hunter. |  Warm-blood. | | |
| **Draught** | No point in this cross. Danger of producing a useless animal. With certain breeds, could get a strong riding school horse, but very much a gamble. |  Draught. | | | |
| **Native** |  Native. | | | | |

## Types and breeds

The Suffolk Punch and Dartmoor are examples of draught and native breeds. Breeding Suffolk with Suffolk or Dartmoor with Dartmoor produces a pure-bred foal of quality and value. However, there is no point in crossing a Suffolk Punch with another draught-horse breed such as a Clydesdale or a Dartmoor with, say, an Exmoor. Cross-breeding two horses that are similar, but from different breeds, clouds the purity of the line and produces a foal that may be sweet but is of little value.

Sometimes breeds are crossed so often and so successfully that the resulting offspring become a breed in their own right. This is the case with the Anglo-Arab, a superb cross between the Thoroughbred and the Arab.

# Body colouring

The colour of a horse is determined by its coat, mane and tail. The main colours are bay, brown, chestnut, black, grey and dun, but there are many variations.

## Take your pick

No one colour is better than another, although many people have preferences. Napoleon, for instance, would only ever ride grey horses. Cowboys used to insist that duns alone had the stamina for cattle-herding, while North Africans consider white horses to be the noblest and blacks the most lucky.

As for coloured (piebald and skewbald) horses, they provoke mixed feelings. Associated with characters of disrepute in olden times in England, they were – by contrast – very popular among Native Americans.

chestnuts

browns

black

bay

cream

dappled grey

strawberry roan

blue roan

spotted

skewbald

palomino

piebald

dun

**Bay:** Dull red, brown or yellowish coat with black mane and tail.

**Black:** All black except for the occasional white markings on the head or legs.

**Brown or Dark Brown:** A mixture of black and brown, with black mane, tail and limbs.

**Chestnut:** Ranges from a light ginger colour to a dark reddish-brown with slightly lighter or darker mane and tail.

**Cream:** Unpigmented skin. Pale chestnut hairs with cream mane and tail.

**Dun:** The body colour is light sand with black mane and tail. Dun ponies have a dark stripe along their backs and occasional zebra markings on their legs.

**Grey:** Black skin with both black and white hairs throughout, the coat varies from light to iron and dappled (mottled).

**Palomino:** The mane and tail are white, the body golden.

**Piebald:** Covered in large, irregular patches of black and white.

**Blue roan:** A black or blue coat is evenly sprinkled with white hairs. The mane and tail are black.

**Strawberry roan or Chestnut roan:** Chestnut and white hairs throughout give a 'pink' appearance.

**Skewbald:** Patches of white and any other colour except black. Both piebalds and skewbalds are known as 'Pintos' in America.

**Spotted:** There are three main types: leopard – white with any colour spots; snowflake – any colour with white spots; blanket – with a spotted rump only.

# Pigmentation of the skin

▲ **Paint horses** have large patches of colour interspersed with areas that have no pigment and are white.

► **Grey colouring** occurs when the coat has a blend of black and white hairs.

★ **THE CREMELLO**
The Cremello is a cream-coloured horse with blue eyes. It carries two genes for its pale colour and is partly albino.

**DID YOU KNOW?**
A horse's skin is protected from the sun by its coat, regardless of the colour. Although they do not like to be too hot, albino horses suffer no more sunburn than those of any other colour.

▼ **This coat pattern** is known as leopard spotted. Patterns depend on many factors, including genes for spots and the colouring of the horse's ancestors.

The first horses to be domesticated were probably dun coloured. All the colours and coat patterns found among modern horses derive from that original sand and black mixture.

## Hair and skin

The colour of a horse is determined by the colour of the hairs that make up its coat. The hair itself is part of the skin and although its length and texture are different it grows in exactly the same way as human hair.

The outermost layer of skin is formed from dead, flattened cells, themselves made from the same substance – keratin – as the horse's hooves. These cells are shed constantly and replaced by the layer of live cells just below.

Beneath these outer layers there is a much thicker layer, with muscles, nerves and glands, well supplied with blood vessels. Among its many functions, the skin helps the body lose heat in the summer and keep warm in winter. In autumn, wild animals accumulate fat in their skin as insulation and it can make the skin rather blue. In summer they lose the fat and the skin becomes a lighter, creamier colour.

Within the layers of skin there are units of cells that produce hairs by stacking cells together to form small tubes. Throughout each hair, scattered at random, there are countless grains of a substance called melanin. It is the melanin that gives the coat colour and without it the coat is white.

## Colour development

Melanin is made in the skin by a series of chemical reactions. It is black, but the products of the reactions that make it are different colours at each stage, going through yellow, orange and red before the process is completed.

Melanin production can be stopped at any stage, or even reversed, so hair can change colour quite naturally. In strong sunlight other chemicals in the skin can bleach the melanin. To make melanin, however, a small amount of copper is needed. If normally dark hair grows paler the diet may be lacking in copper.

When an animal grows old some areas in its skin may stop producing melanin, so hairs nearby turn white. Mixed among dark hairs they produce a grey colour. It happens to humans and it

## Eye colour

Horses with genes for pale colour sometimes have blue eyes. This is because melanin not only decides the colour of the coat, but also that of the eyes. Blue eyes occur where there is no melanin to colour them. A horse with genes for normal melanin production has brown eyes.

★ **ALBINOISM**
Some individuals, in all animal species, carry genes that prevent melanin production altogether. An individual inheriting such a gene may be pale, possibly with blue eyes.

A horse that inherits two such genes, one from each parent, is albino. Albinos are pure white, sometimes with such pale eyes that their blood vessels tint them pink.

happens to horses. The hair can go grey, and eventually white, in old age. Injury to the skin can also make hairs turn white, usually in patches where damaged tissue has lost its ability to make melanin.

## *Paints on a palette*

Melanin production is controlled by 'genes'. They determine the amount of melanin produced and at which stage the chemical reactions stop. A foal inherits these characteristics from its parents. If the sire and dam are different colours the foal's coat may resemble one of them or a mixture of the two.

With the wide range of natural shades of white (no melanin), yellow, orange, red, brown and black, cross-breeding is like mixing paints on a palette.

▲ **Palomino colouring** can be achieved by crossing a Cremello stallion with a chestnut mare.

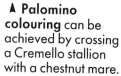

◄ **Appaloosas** can have a variety of coat patterns. This one is known as 'blanket' coated. The body is coloured except for areas on the hindquarters, which are left white.

# Head and leg markings

It is not always possible to identify a horse simply by describing its colour. Instead, you may need to talk about its age, sex, height and – most helpful of all – its markings.

## Every horse unique

Nearly all domestic horses have some kind of marking (a patch of white hair, often on the legs or face). Markings can vary in shape and size and no two horses are ever exactly the same.

This means that the pattern of markings on a horse's body are his own unique record and are a great help for identification purposes.

On the face, you might find a small white 'snip' between the nostrils or an entirely white, mask-like pattern which is known as a white (or bald) face. Leg markings are equally varied and include anything from a splash of white on the heel to an entire leg, where the white hair may extend from the coronet right up the leg and beyond the hock.

Markings are not just found on the face or legs. In some breeds, like the Clydesdale, they are also common on the belly or the hindquarters.

snip

stripe

flower-shaped star

star

crown

coronet

half pastern

pastern

fetlock

blaze

white face

white to stifle
in front and
above hock
behind

white knee

white muzzle

white leg

heel

fleck

white to hock

white to knee

white to
proximal fetlock

**Blaze:** A broad white band which runs the length of the face.

**Coronet:** A thin rim around the top of the hoof.

**Crown:** A semi-circle above the front of the hoof.

**Fetlock:** White hair from coronet to fetlock.

**Fleck:** A small irregular patch of white hairs.

**Flower:** This star resembles a flower shape.

**Heel:** A small patch above the rear of the hoof.

**Knee:** This reaches from hoof to knee.

**Leg:** Marking covers the whole leg. The hooves are often unpigmented (white).

**Pastern:** Extends from the hoof to the tip of the pastern.

**Snip:** A patch between the nostrils.

**Star:** Any white mark on the forehead. The exact shape, size and position should be described.

**Stripe:** A thin white line of hairs from forehead to muzzle which may join on to the star.

**White face:** A patch across the face which covers the eyes and runs towards the mouth.

**White muzzle:** This covers the nostrils, the muzzle and, usually, the upper and lower lips.

Terms such as **sock, stocking,** etc are seldom used. All markings on the limbs are described using the points of the anatomy, eg **white to fetlock, white to mid-cannon,** or **white patch on coronet – outside.**

**21**

# Face value

Apart from identical twins, no two horses look exactly alike, any more than two humans do. Each is an individual with his own character, and this shows in his face. And – if you know what to look for – his ancestry is there, too.

## Face facts

The shape of a horse's face is handed down from generation to generation so it is an indication of his origins.

The nasal (nose) bone – just below the skin – gives the face its shape and forms the upper part of the airway, which leads from the nostrils down to the lungs.

In horses today there are two distinctive types of face.

**Dished:** Here the line of the nose is hollowed, as in a pure-bred Arab.
**Convex:** Here the line of the nose curves outward and can either be arched or Roman. An arched nose curves outward for the whole of its length. A nose that starts straight but curves downward sharply toward the nostrils is Roman.

In between these two extremes fall many other types, including the straight nose – which is the most common – and the undulating, where the face is dished near the eyes but then curves outward.

## How it all began

Thousands of years ago, wild horses in northern Europe were heavily built,

▼ **Face shapes** vary from dished to Roman, but the majority of horses come somewhere in between these two extremes – this champion riding pony has a straight face.

with large heads, and their noses tended to be arched or Roman. Their descendants are draught horses, such as the Shire, who have retained the characteristically shaped faces.

Although not a heavy horse, the Andalusian from Spain also had a Roman nose, and as one of the original races it, too, has had a strong influence on the faces of today's breeds.

On the other hand, the horses which lived in the hot desert lands of the Middle East were lightly built. With their long narrow faces and rather straight or dished noses they gave rise to the modern-day Arab.

All these horses have inter-bred to produce the different faces seen today.

## Face make-up

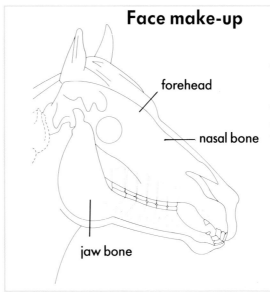

Face shapes are decided by the nasal (nose) bone. It lies just below the skin and forms the upper side of the airway leading from the nostrils to the lungs.

The jaw bone (mandible) is big and powerful, and allows plenty of room for the horse's teeth, which have to be large for crushing food to a pulp.

## Face shapes

**The most common profile** starts straightish and then curves downward toward the nostrils.

**A Roman nose** has a convex profile. This is typical of many draught horses.

**A dished face** is one where the line of the nose is hollowed (concave). The best known example is a pure-bred Arab.

**An undulating face** is dished near the eyes, but then curves outward.

# Life history

The life expectancy of a domesticated horse is about 25 years – for a horse in the wild, it is slightly less. From birth to death, the horse's life is a series of milestones.

## Under threes

The horse is very well developed from the moment he enters the world. Within 24 hours of birth, a foal in the wild has to be able to gallop with the herd if he is to survive. For this reason, he has very long legs (nearly their adult length) and an instinct to get up and start moving as soon as he is born.

During his first month of life, a foal's height increases by about a third. By the end of his first year, he is three-quarters of his adult height.

After weaning, which happens at about six months old in domestication and slightly later in the wild, a youngster is called a weanling. On his first birthday, he becomes known as a yearling. After this, he is a two-year-old, a three-year-old, and so on.

A horse is broken in at about three years of age. Youngsters must be trained gently and gradually because stress can shorten their lives.

## Work begins

Most horses are fully mature at the age of six. If he is to have a long working life, a horse must not be put to hard work until he is fully mature.

▲ **Although they look out of proportion,** foals have long legs so that they can keep up with the herd from birth. A foal tries to stand up within minutes of being born, and can canter confidently alongside his mother when he is only a few days old.

►**Yearlings** are three-quarters of their adult height. They haven't quite filled out yet so they look rather lanky.

◄ **This three-year-old** has reached his adult size and is ready to begin training. He learns to accept a rider through patient training on the lunge.

**Overleaf:** Racehorses reach their peak as three-year-olds. They are trained as two-year-olds and race for a couple of seasons before retiring and finding new jobs as riding horses or as sires for the next generation of racehorses.

Racehorses are different. They often work their hardest as three-year-olds. This is because racehorses are bred to mature early. At the age of four, the average racehorse retires to stud. If his career is cut short by injury before then, he is sometimes used to sire foals, or he may find new work as a riding horse if he is fit enough.

## Old age
A horse starts to grow old when he is about 15. From then on, his body systems work less efficiently than before. He loses his strength and finds he cannot work as hard as when he was young. But he is still good for many years, provided that he is given a suitable diet, has plenty of regular, gentle exercise and is well clothed and sheltered in winter.

Domesticated horses are rarely left to die in pain. They are put down rather than allowed to suffer. It is kindest if the vet comes to the horse while he is in his stable, so that he dies in familiar surroundings.

In the wild, horses die slightly younger than in domestication because life is harder with no veterinary attention and the threat of predators. When a horse senses that death is near, he may leave the herd to be on his own and die in peace.

▼ **As a horse grows older,** he slows down and finds it harder to do the tasks he used to be able to do easily. During old age a horse needs more care and attention from his owner to make sure he's comfortable.

# The first year

Unlike a newborn baby, a foal can stand and walk within a few hours of its birth. After a few days, it can run fast enough to keep up with its mother.

## The need to escape

Nowadays, most horses are domesticated and have no fear of other animals. But, in the wild, they are just one link in nature's food chain and must protect themselves against predators like wild cats and dogs.

When foals are born their legs are already 90% of their adult length so that youngsters are instantly equipped for speed – and can escape from danger by running away.

Young horses are naturally inquisitive and eager to learn about their surroundings. They enjoy playing and charge around investigating all the new sights and smells and testing the strength of their legs. This helps to build up their muscles but they soon get tired. To make up for all their skittish activity, regular periods of sleep are essential. Plenty of rest helps 'recharge the batteries' and ensures that the foal is healthy and happy.

## Rate of growth

For the first five years of life, one year for a horse equals five human years. So a six-month-old foal is at the same stage of development as a two-and-a-half-year-old child.

▼ **Although a foal's body** is relatively small, its legs are almost the same length as its mother's.

The long legs enable the foal to run quickly so that it can keep up with the herd and escape from any potential danger.

◄ **A mare** gets to know her foal just after the birth. A new mother is usually very protective of her foal and, for the first few days, should be given as much peace and quiet as possible.

Once the foal is old enough to be playful, the mare's headcollar must be properly fitted.

◄ **Like most youngsters,** foals have bundles of energy. Exercise develops healthy muscles in the legs — which are always a bit wobbly at first!

Unlike humans, however, a foal achieves about three quarters of its total growth in its first year. During the first four weeks, its height increases by about a third. Development slows slightly, then between six and 12 months the foal shoots up again. Its body fills out and its girth measurement increases.

You can estimate the mature height of a foal when it is three months old. Measure in inches from the point of the elbow to the ground. Halve the number of inches and you have the approximate height in hands. So, a foal which measures 28 inches will be about 14 hands high – as long as it doesn't have any setbacks. Foals who are deprived of exercise and good food, particularly during the first month of life, suffer from bad health and never achieve their full potential height or strength.

A hungry youngster looks tired and thin and stays close to its mother, constantly trying to feed. By contrast, a contented foal is well-rounded, has a shiny coat and spends its life feeding, sleeping and, of course, playing!

► **Friendship** is extremely important to ponies. These Welsh pony foals spend much of their time playing and resting together.

# The second year

Although growth in yearlings – horses between 12 and 23 months old – is less dramatic than in foals, a one-year-old shows distinct changes in development and behaviour.

## Growing up

From the age of one, a horse's body begins to fill out and starts to catch up with its long legs. The hindquarters, which provide drive and power, increase in strength and become more muscular. As this 'engine room' develops, yearlings can canter and gallop at a reasonable speed but still lack the strength and endurance of more mature horses.

In their first autumn, the youngsters lose their fluffy foal coats and the short, soft hair in their manes and tails is replaced by 'proper' hair. This more grown-up appearance can lead to quite dramatic changes and the new coat may be a completely different colour from the old one! A dun foal may, for example, become either bay or brown unless it is a true dun – with black legs, mane and tail and a dark stripe along the backbone. It is also quite common for a chestnut foal to turn grey if it has one grey parent.

▼ Playing is a favourite pastime for yearlings. Games are quite competitive and are an indication of fights for dominance in later life.

Although horses are not sexually mature until the age of three, yearlings can serve (mate with) females and get them in foal. So yearlings should always be kept away from mares when turned out in a field.

### Competition time

As they play together, yearlings are more boisterous and more competitive than foals. They are weaned from their dams (mothers) and usually have no adult horse among them to keep order: instead, they must establish their own pecking order and decide who is boss!

## Croup high

In yearlings, the highest point of the hindquarters — the croup — is usually above the highest point of the forehand — the withers. This conformation (shown by the red line on the right) is called 'croup high', and is normal in youngsters.

The hindquarters develop earlier because, like an engine, they provide the power to drive a horse forward. This makes the yearling look out of proportion for a while.

The withers and croup usually even up at the age of three or four. But in some horses they never catch up. These mounts give their riders the feeling that they are going downhill all the time — not a very pleasant experience!

▲ **The body** begins to fill out and catch up with the long hindlegs, but the face still looks young.

▼ **Yearlings are** still developing their speed, although they may look full of energy. They are not yet strong enough to run for long periods of time.

# Learning about life

A foal is born knowing just enough to survive, with the help of his mother. Most of life is still a mystery to him, and as he grows up he has to learn how to live by trial and error.

### Early lessons
Very soon after a foal is born, he manages to stand and suckle. Before long he can recognize his mother by her smell and voice, then he comes to know the other members of the herd, too.

From all the horses in his social group, the foal learns how to behave and how to communicate. The meaning of body postures, gestures and sounds slowly becomes clear to him.

### Self-taught
As he gets bigger, the foal has to find his own food. He discovers by experiment which plants are good to eat and remembers their flavour by their smell. With practice he learns to save time, by searching for food and water by scent.

A little more confident now, the foal is keen to explore. Horses are naturally good at finding their way, and he soon begins to make a mental map of his surroundings. He learns the shortest route from A to B and takes note of the best places to graze, drink, rest and hide from danger.

### Knowing good from bad
Throughout his early explorations, a young horse spends much of the time fleeing from danger – it is his sole form of

▲ **A foal** quickly learns to recognize his mother and sticks close by her for protection.

►**Youngsters** prepare themselves for adult life by spending time with older horses and copying them.

defence. He works from the sensible assumption that everything is dangerous until proved otherwise. Only with time does he learn to distinguish what is safe from what is hazardous.

Pleasant and unpleasant experiences are often associated for him with places. (This is especially true if he is a hot-blood.) When something good happens at a particular spot, he remembers it and goes back there. When something bad happens, he avoids the place – often to the bewilderment of his rider, who probably wasn't there when his horse originally took fright. If the impression made on him is really strong, the memory may last his whole life long.

## Into training

A horse learns to live with man in the same way as he does with his fellow horses. He soon comes to recognize his trainer's voice, for instance.

To train a horse, man has to persuade him to alter slightly what he has learned for himself. Although it's impossible to teach a horse to perform tasks that are completely alien to him, it is possible to cheat – so that what he does naturally serves a quite different human purpose. In the wild, for example, horses never charge at one another or hunt other animals. Man, however, fights and hunts on horseback – with the help of horses who have learned to trust and obey his commands.

▲ **Young horses** love to explore. By making mental maps of their surroundings they can always find their way back to the herd if they stray too far.

◀ **A horse** can be persuaded to alter his natural skills. In the wild, horses never race, but trained by man they can be urged to run their fastest if they have a bold character.

# The middle years

A horse is usually fully mature when he is six years old. By then, he has reached his full height and his bones are fully grown.

## Filling out

The main change you'll notice in a horse's appearance is a general filling out of his body. This is because his muscles have developed. He looks bigger and more imposing, but without getting any taller.

His adult life should be long and productive as long as he has been well looked after during his early years.

## Strength and stamina

The speed a horse builds up as a youngster reaches its greatest point between the years of two and six. From then on, his actual speed lessens but is replaced by increased strength and stamina.

He *gets* fit more quickly than a young or old horse and *stays* fit longer without needing a rest or holiday.

## The prime of life

A horse's 'teenage' years, in human terms, are from three to five. After he is six years old, you can reckon that one

▼ Filling out: As the horse gets older and does more work, his body becomes broader and more muscular. This makes him seem larger even though he's already reached his full adult height.

year to us equals three to a horse. So, from six to 14, he's at roughly the same stage as a person of 18 to 45.

A horse is at his peak, in the prime of life, between eight and 12-14. These middle years are often a horse's healthiest. He is no longer plagued so much by the health problems of the young – teething, strangles, jarred limbs, warts, breathing diseases. But he hasn't yet succumbed to the disorders of the elderly either.

Provided his work is sensibly balanced, it is difficult to overburden a fit, healthy and well-cared-for horse at this time of life.

## Fully formed

Once the word 'teen' appears in a horse's age, some people feel he is getting past his best. But many horses continue to work eagerly and productively even after the age of 14.

Technically, a horse is said to be 'aged' when he is eight years old. Aged in this sense doesn't necessarily mean old, just that you can no longer tell his age accurately.

At the age of eight, a horse's character is fully developed and he knows about the world. His outlook on life – whether sensible, calm and wise or nervous, excitable and scatty – is unlikely to change much now.

▲ **Speed gives way** to strength and stamina; a horse can work harder now than at any other time in his life.

◄ **Worldly wise:** By the age of eight, a horse has learnt a lot about life, and his character is formed.

▼ **Horses** in the prime of life are usually at their healthiest, free of the problems of the young and old.

# The last years

Physically, horses in their 20's are past their best, but mentally they are often in better shape than their younger counterparts.

## Schoolmasters

For many purposes, older horses are better than younger ones: they are experienced and usually sensible and unruffled by any situation.

They can make excellent 'schoolmaster' animals, being patient and steady enough for beginners to learn to ride on them. They show young horses the ropes when out hacking, giving a lead over tricky places and in traffic. And, when travelling, they have a calming influence on ponies who are nervous about being boxed.

## Growing old

The average lifespan for a horse is 25 years, although it has been known for them to live much longer than this. A Cleveland cross-breed called 'Old Billy', born in 1760, is said to have lived to the remarkable age of 62!

Ponies tend to live longer than horses. A 20-year old pony is about equal to a 70-year old human, a 30-year old pony to a 100-year old human.

▼ **Just because a** horse gets old doesn't mean you can't ride him any more. Indeed, regular (almost daily), steady exercise is much better for him than little or no work.

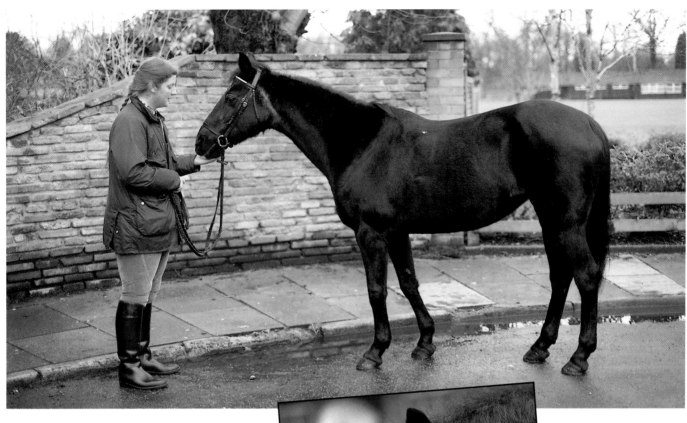

Older horses cannot work as hard or for as long as young ones. But regular, light exercise keeps them healthier than occasional work or none at all.

Like all old animals, horses feel their age sooner or later. They become slower and stiffer as their joints lose mobility, and their limbs and body in general lose their youthful suppleness. Because of this it becomes increasingly difficult for horses to lie down and stand up again, so they often prefer to stand while resting.

### Body matters

Older horses are likely to suffer from disorders such as arthritis and rheumatism, and the circulation and digestion begin to deteriorate. As the teeth begin to wear down, old horses commonly suffer from dental problems.

The horse's outward appearance also changes. Some old horses start to lose weight. Careful management of work and feeding is required to prevent them from losing condition, especially in the winter, when they feel the cold more.

The back may sink down a little, and the legs bend slightly forward at the knees and sink lower at the fetlocks.

The colour of the coat can change – for example, a grey pony lightens with age. Other colours may produce grey hairs in the coat, particularly on the head – giving a grizzled, slightly 'dusty' look.

▲ Slightly bent knees are a common feature of old age, as the leg joints stiffen up.

◄ Just like humans, some horses go grey as they get older.

▼ It is often hard to tell if a pony is old just by looking at him. A hollow (dipped) back is a good clue.

PART TWO

THE
SENSES

# All about teeth

The horse's teeth are well designed to cope with his main source of food – grass. Although constant chewing and grinding of grass wears away the tooth surface, horses' teeth continue to grow throughout their lives – unlike ours, which do not grow at all once they have fully developed. Growth normally occurs in a tooth at the same rate at which it is being worn away. This means that the teeth always *appear* to be the same, unchanging length.

## How the teeth work

The horse's teeth begin the digestive process by cutting and crushing the food, so it is in a suitable state for the rest of the digestive system to work on. A horse's front teeth (incisors) act like very sharp scissors, cutting the grass and enabling the animal to graze very close to the ground.

After it has been cut, the grass is transferred to the back of the mouth by the tongue, which is very mobile. Here the grass is thoroughly ground between the cheek teeth before being swallowed.

## The horse's teeth

All adult horses have at least 36 teeth – 12 front teeth (incisors) and 24 cheek teeth (molars). Male horses usually have four extra teeth, called 'tushes' (canines).
**The front teeth (incisors):** There are six incisor teeth in each jaw (upper and lower). They must meet exactly for the animal to eat effectively. When the upper teeth are in front of the lower ones ('parrot' mouth), or the other way round ('under-shot'), it is difficult for the animal to graze properly.
**Cheek teeth (premolars and molars):** There are six cheek teeth on each side of the upper jaw, and the same number in the lower jaw. Technically, there are three

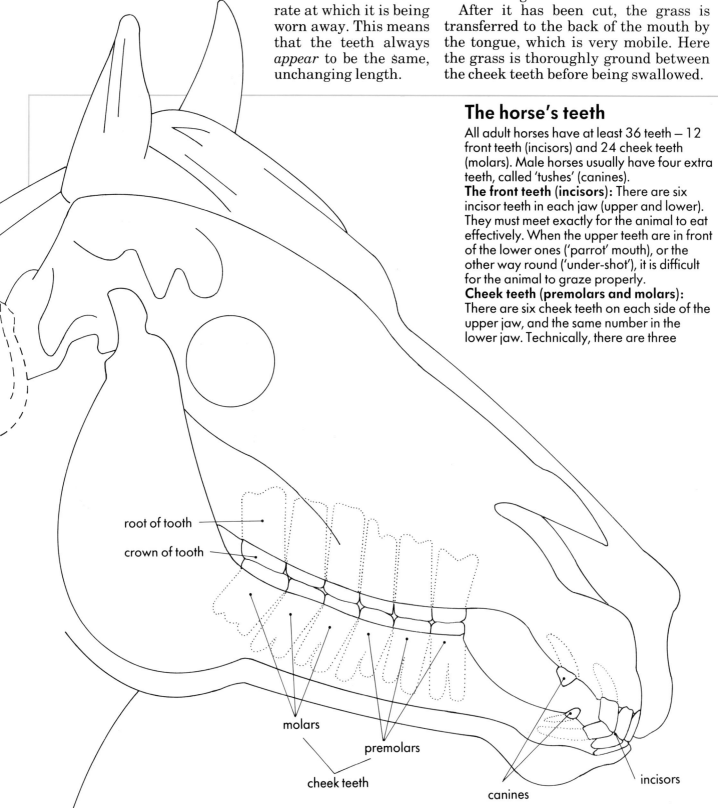

root of tooth

crown of tooth

molars

premolars

cheek teeth

canines

incisors

► **Not just for eating:** These two horses are using their teeth for mutual grooming. This is where they scratch each other's withers, back or the top of the tail. Not only does this relieve itching in difficult-to-reach places, but it is a sign of friendship and trust.

*premolar* teeth and three *molar* teeth, but there is no real difference between them.

These teeth are covered with a hard substance called enamel, but the grinding surface is folded into many ridges and crevices in which there is an even harder material known as cement.

**Canine teeth (tushes):** Stallions and geldings usually develop small canine teeth at four years old, but three out of four mares do not possess them at all. They are found in the space between the front teeth and the cheek teeth. As they do not meet with the same tooth in the opposite jaw, they cannot be used for eating, and may become quite sharp.

## Teeth and diet

The horse is a *herbivore* (he eats grass and other vegetation) and the tiger is a *carnivore* (meat-eater). Because of their opposite diets, their teeth are shaped completely differently. The horse's incisors (front teeth) are well-developed chisels for cutting grass — unlike those of the tiger, which are tiny and of little importance. In contrast, the tiger has large, pointed canines for catching and holding prey. The horse's canines are either small or absent because they have no eating function.

## Prehistoric teeth

The earliest prehistoric horses lived in swamps some 60-70 million years ago. Here they ate juicy fruits and succulent plants. These animals had very small, soft teeth which were well suited to their diet. Over millions of years, the climate changed. The swamps were replaced by dry plains where there was only a sparse covering of much tougher food material – grass.

During this period the teeth of the horse's ancestors gradually altered to cope with their new diet. The small soft teeth were replaced by much bigger ones with a tougher grinding surface. The horse's facial bones lengthened to make room for these large teeth. Powerful jaw muscles also developed, so the horse could crush the grass to pulp.

## Wolf teeth

A few horses have extra, tiny cheek teeth, known as 'wolf' teeth. They lie in front of the upper cheek teeth and, rarely, in front of the lower cheek teeth as well.

These teeth can be very sharp. When the bit pulls the horse's cheeks against them, the cheeks may be cut and become sore. This can make the horse unwilling to respond to his rider's instructions. So these 'useless' teeth are sometimes removed by the vet, under a painless local anaesthetic.

**RASPING THE TEETH**
If the surface of the tooth wears down unevenly, the edges may become sharp and cut the cheeks and tongue, so the horse cannot chew his food properly.

When this happens, a vet must 'rasp' the teeth (file them down to make the surfaces level). Tooth problems are very common in old horses, and their teeth should be checked regularly.

# Telling a horse's age

Horses' front teeth (incisors) show characteristic signs of wear with age. These changes can be used to tell a pony's age fairly accurately up to the age of 8. Beyond this, it is only possible to give an estimate, so horses and ponies over 8 are often described as 'aged'.

## Milk teeth

A pony has a full set of six temporary *(milk)* incisor teeth in each jaw by the time he is 9 months old. The two innermost teeth in each jaw are called *centrals*, those on each side of them are called *laterals* (or *middle* incisors), and those at the corners of the mouth are known as *corners*.

Between 2½ and 4½ years, the temporary teeth are replaced by permanent ones. You should be able to distinguish the white, shell-like milk teeth from the bigger, yellowish, adult ones, when ageing young horses.

## The tables

The next step is to inspect the grinding surfaces of the teeth (called *tables*). The outline of the tables changes with age – it is oval in young horses (5 years), becomes circular by 8, then more and more triangular.

In the middle of the tables of young horses is a hole known as the *infundibulum*. As the teeth wear down, this hole becomes less obvious and eventually disappears. Wear also exposes a

---

### Birth to 4 weeks

The two innermost temporary incisors ('centrals') are either present at birth, or emerge soon afterwards. These teeth have a large hole in the centre – the *infundibulum*.

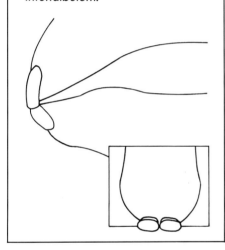

---

### 4 to 6 weeks

The second pair of temporary incisors ('laterals' or middle incisors) have now emerged through the gums on each side of the centrals.

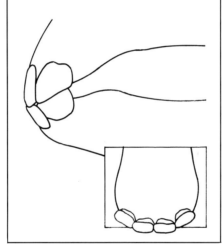

---

### 6 to 9 months

The third pair of temporary incisors ('corners') come through at about 9 months, but are not 'fully in wear' (meet with the opposite teeth) until 3 to 5 months later.

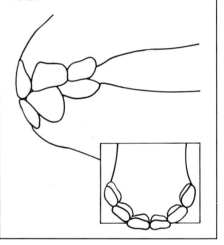

---

### 6 years

The infundibulum has become faint and has almost disappeared from the central teeth. Up to this age, the central incisors meet vertically.

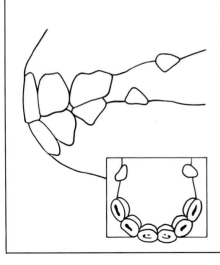

---

### 7 years

The upper corner incisors have developed the typical '7 year hook'. The centrals are becoming rounder in outline than the oval shape of younger horses.

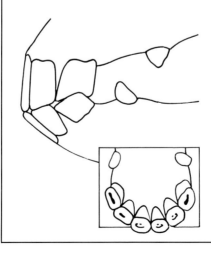

---

### 8 years

The black *dental star* is becoming apparent, just in front of the remains of the infundibulum in the centrals and laterals. The teeth now meet at an angle, not vertically.

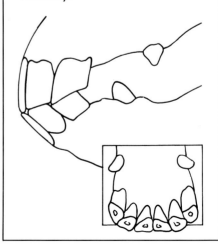

ridge of dentine which is first seen as a black, elongated line in front of the infundibulum at 8 years. This is known as the *dental star*. It becomes progressively more circular as the horse gets older.

## Long in the tooth

In young horses (up to 8 years) the teeth meet vertically when viewed from the side. Beyond the age of 8, the angle between upper and lower teeth becomes in-creasingly more acute, until, at 20, the teeth meet at right angles. In old horses, too, the gums recede from the teeth – they become 'long in the tooth'.

In some horses and ponies (but not all) there is a stained groove on the outer surface of the upper corner incisors. This is known as *Galvayne's groove*. It first appears at the gum at 10, has grown half way down the tooth by 15, and reaches the grinding surface at 20.

**Looking at teeth:** a tricky business!

### 3 years

The temporary central incisors are replaced by larger, permanent ones at 2½ years old, but these do not come fully into wear until the horse is 3.

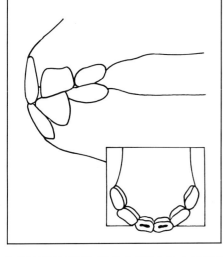

### 4 years

The temporary lateral (middle) incisors have been lost and replaced by permanent ones at 3½. They will not come fully into wear until the horse is 4 years old.

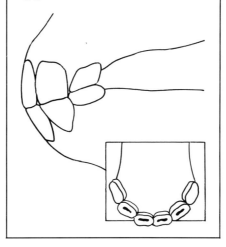

### 4½ years

The temporary corner incisors are being replaced by permanent ones. The pony will have a complete set of adult teeth when he is 5. The canine teeth ('tushes') have emerged after 4.

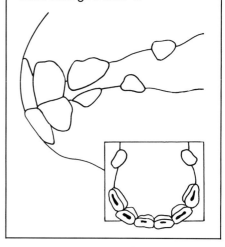

### 10 years

Dental stars are present in all teeth. The centrals are becoming more triangular in outline. *Galvayne's groove* is just appearing at the gum on the upper corner teeth.

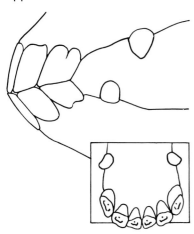

### 13 years

The infundibulum has just about disappeared from all six teeth. The dental stars are becoming wider and rounder. The teeth are more triangular in outline, and meet at a much greater angle.

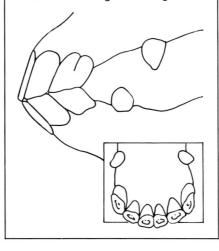

### 20 years

The angle between the two sets of teeth is now almost 90°. The tables are triangular in outline, and Galvayne's groove has reached the tip of the upper corner teeth.

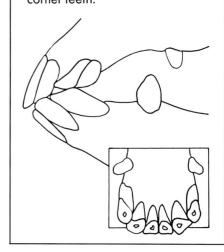

# Sight and hearing

In the wild, a horse is naturally defensive. When threatened, his instinct is to escape. But he needs advance warning to run away in enough time to avoid the danger.

The horse's eyes and ears work together to give this warning. The eyes are geared for sideways vision, backed up by acute hearing.

## Seeing sideways

Horses have prominent eyes which are set well apart on the sides of the face. This means that a horse can see almost all around his body with one or other eye and can detect danger.

However, this eye position presents a problem. Most of a horse's vision is one eyed and he cannot see directly in front or behind – he has a blind spot.

## The sensitive ear

To help their sight, horses have extremely sensitive hearing. They can locate the *exact* source of sound, picking up softer noises than the human ear.

A horse has 16 muscles controlling each ear and can move his ears separately toward the sound, rather than moving the whole head. The funnel shape of the ears helps to make sounds seem louder and clearer.

▼ **The position of a horse's eyes** limits sight directly in front and behind.

When a horse looks straight ahead with his head in its normal resting position, the eyes focus on a point about 2m (7ft) from his muzzle. A horse cannot see immediately in front of him. This area is known as the blind spot.

► **Horses sometimes wear blinkers** in harness to restrict their sideways vision.

Blinkers stop a horse being distracted from the work in hand and help to keep his concentration.

▼ **Horses cannot focus** on obstacles straight in front of them.

If a horse cannot see or remember a fence, he may refuse to jump (below). Once he has investigated the obstacle (below right), he should jump clear.

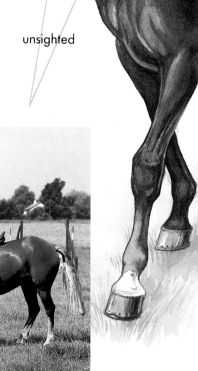

sight with right eye only

unsighted

◄ **When startled** by a strange or unusual noise a horse often prepares for flight. He pricks up his ears, points them toward the sound (left), tries to identify it and then decides whether or not he needs to take flight (below).

unsighted

sight with left eye only

► **Horses can move their ears** to point in every direction around their body.

This mare points her ears backward to check what is behind her, so that she is always ready to protect her foal. The foal in turn listens to his mother to check that everything is safe.

# How the horse hears

The horse has excellent hearing. His ears are extremely mobile as they have 16 muscles to move them. This allows the horse to 'catch' sound from the air all around him.

## Collecting sound

Sound is made up of vibrations in the air. The funnel-shaped *pinna* (outer ear) moves around to collect these vibrations. From there they pass along a hollow tube to the *ear drum*. This is a taut membrane, just like the skin on a drum, and it vibrates when sound strikes it.

Behind the ear drum lies the *middle ear*, a hollow, air-filled space in the skull. The middle ear contains three small bones called the *hammer, anvil* and *stirrup*. They are loosely connected to one another and the hammer is attached to the inside of the ear drum. When the drum vibrates so do the bones, and the stirrup transmits the sound through to the *inner ear* chamber.

Situated in the inner ear is a structure called the *cochlea*, which is connected to the stirrup. The cochlea is coiled, rather like a snail's shell, and is made up of fluid-filled membranes.

When the stirrup vibrates, the pressure changes in the fluid of the cochlea. This is picked up by fine, hair-like growths, which project from cells in the cochlea membrane. These cells are richly supplied with nerves. When the hairs vibrate, the movement is converted into nerve impulses that travel directly to the brain. Here the nerve impulses are converted again into messages that the animal can recognize as sounds.

## Balance

The inner ear sits deep in the skull and is very delicate. Within the inner ear there are passages made from thin membrane and filled with fluid. Three of these passages are semi-circular in shape and set at right angles. They control balance.

▼ **As horses approach** you, their large, flexible ears are pricked, rather like antennae tuned to receive incoming signals.

**Overleaf:** Mother and foal have been startled by a noise behind them. As they move away, the mare's ears point backward in an attempt to identify the sound.

**! PROTECTIVE**
**● HAIRS**
The hairs just inside the horse's ears are for protection. They stop insects, seeds and dust particles going into the ear and causing damage. Avoid trimming these hairs as they have an important part to play.

▲ **The funnel-shaped outer ears** collect sounds from the air. They have protective hairs inside to filter out any tiny particles, such as dust or seeds, that could enter the delicate parts of the ears and cause damage.

▼ **The horse's ears** are well supplied with muscles. He can turn each one of them separately so that he doesn't miss anything that's going on around him.

## Sensitive ears

A horse relies on his keen sense of hearing for survival. He can detect sounds that are much too quiet for human hearing. His ears prick up attentively at the approach of something his rider can't hear until it is much closer. He can also hear sounds that are too high pitched for the human ear to detect.

Just like people though, horses lose their ability to hear very high-pitched sounds as they grow older.

## Ear conformation

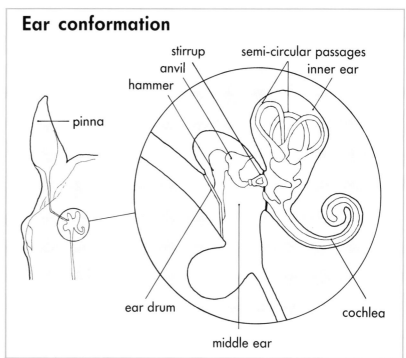

pinna

stirrup
anvil
hammer

semi-circular passages
inner ear

ear drum

cochlea

middle ear

47

# A good look round

► **A horse** has a wide field of vision — even with his head down, he can keep a look-out around him.

Horses are herbivores and so must have their heads down at grass level for much of the time. Because of this, the horse has specially adapted eyesight which means he can keep watch for predators even as he eats.

## All-round vision

A horse's eyes are set on each side of the head and can see independently of one another — in a wide arc to the left and in a wide arc to the right. Only when the horse looks directly ahead does he focus with both eyes at once.

The combined information from this 'sideways' arrangement gives the horse an almost complete picture of what is happening everywhere around him.

From this picture, the horse can identify movements and the outlines of possible predators before they approach too closely.

His sideways vision does have one drawback however: the horse needs to look at an object with both eyes before he can tell exactly how close or far away it is. In the wild, this does not present any problems. When the horse wants to jump, say, a stream, he is already looking forward and using both eyes so he can judge the distance perfectly.

## Sympathetic riding

Bad riding or badly fitting tack is often the cause of a horse jumping poorly. If his head movements are seriously hampered, the horse cannot get a good look at the obstacle or measure his stride pattern to it. A good rider should also understand why a horse shies away from something to his side: the horse cannot see it clearly and his instinctive reaction is to get away. This is probably a survival response inherited from the horse's ancestors, who lived in the wild and needed to react quickly at the approach of predators.

## Eye conformation

A horse's eyes are adapted for scanning large areas at the same time: they are on the side of the head so the horse can see sideways with each eye. The wide angle of vision is increased by the horizontal slit shape of the pupil (the eye's opening, through which light passes). The black area on the edge of the pupil is called the corpora nigra. It narrows to shield the pupil in bright sunlight.

To focus on something a horse looks through the upper part of the front of the eye (the cornea). Light enters the cornea and passes through the lens on to the retina.

From the retina, messages are sent along the optic nerve to the brain, and here they can be 'translated'. A horse's eyes are protected, like humans', by upper and lower eyelids with lashes.

▼ **It's difficult** to imagine how the world looks through a horse's eyes. You can get some idea, however, by studying the landscape below. A **human** standing at point X would naturally focus on the scene immediately ahead — here a horse grazing — and see very little to either side.

A **horse** standing at point X would have a different image. He can either focus on the horse in front of him, or see a broad sweep of countryside to either side.

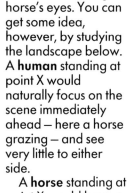

## The horse's field of vision

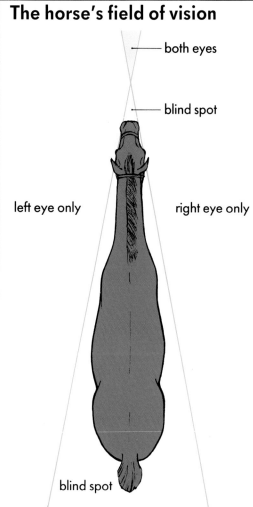

both eyes

blind spot

left eye only

right eye only

blind spot

### JUDGING DISTANCE

You can do your own simple experiment to understand why a horse must focus both eyes *together* when judging distance.

Put any small object in front of you and just beyond arm's reach. Then cover one eye with the palm of your hand and try to pick up the object with your other hand. Repeat the exercise without covering either eye and you'll find it's much easier.

Apart from a small area directly behind, a horse can see everything around him.

Each eye can see for slightly less than half a circle. But the area the horse can see in front of him, covered by *both* eyes, is much *smaller*. It is only in this area that he can judge accurately how far something is away from him. To judge distances 'to the side', he has to turn his head in that direction.

There are certain areas that he cannot see at all without turning his head: directly behind him, the ground for about 120cm (4ft) in front (the nose gets in the way!) and the ground immediately under him.

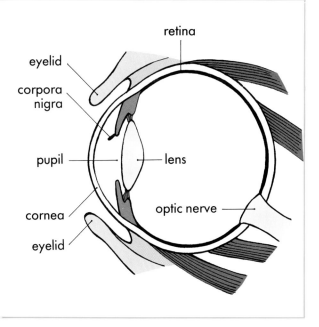

retina

eyelid

corpora nigra

pupil

lens

cornea

optic nerve

eyelid

human
horse

# Smell and taste

The senses of smell and taste play a very important part in the lives of horses because they act as a warning system. Smell is useful for sorting out the familiar from the unknown and taste helps a horse to distinguish between healthy and harmful food or water.

## Recognizing each other

A horse uses its acute sense of smell to investigate strange objects. When a pony enters an unfamiliar stable or paddock the first thing he does is sniff and snort at his new surroundings.

Horses recognize their friends and rivals through body smell – each individual has its own scent. Horses usually sniff each other's breath when they greet one another. This is the equine equivalent of a hand-shake.

Scent is particularly important in the bond between mare and foal. A mare works out which foal belongs to her by the smell it gives off.

Horses even get used to a person's natural odour and any unusual smell such as perfume confuses them and can upset them.

When a horse wants to study a smell more closely, he takes a deep breath, raises his head and curls the top lip upward, over the nostrils, to trap the smell in his nose. This behaviour is known as 'flehmen'.

## In the wild

Horses can detect smells over long distances. A stallion can pick up the scent of a mare that is in season when she is up to 600m (780yds) away. Horses can tell where there is water from a long way away as well.

Smells also form a part of boundary marking. Horses deposit droppings and urine around their personal territory so that others can recognize the borders and avoid 'trespassing'.

A horse's strong sense of smell discourages it from grazing near droppings because they send out an unpleasant odour. This is important in preventing the spread of worms.

## The sweet tooth

Horses choose their food firstly by smell and then by taste. Their muzzles act like

▲ **Treat your horse** to sweet titbits every now and then. But try not to give him too many because he'll expect them all the time and it may make him bad mannered.

➤ **Smell** is one of the horse's most important senses. A horse recognizes his friends by their body smell. Here a couple of wild horses sniff each other's breath in recognition.

fingers in helping to sort out what they want to eat and what they want to leave behind.

Having passed the 'sniff' test, food can then be distinguished by its sweet, bitter, sour or salty taste. Generally horses dislike bitter tastes and have a sweet tooth.

Because of this, they usually love sugar lumps and are often fond of soaked sugar beet. They also like unusual or spicy tastes, including peppermints and ginger.

The 'taste' test is a final safety mechanism: poisonous plants, such as ragwort, yew and laburnum, taste extremely bitter and are quickly rejected. Even if a horse or pony is tempted to take a bite of something dangerous, in most cases he spits it out straight away.

▲ **Although horses do not eat buttercups** from choice, they sometimes munch them with a mouthful of grass because these flowers do not taste as bitter as other poisonous plants. Fortunately buttercups are only harmful if they are eaten in great quantities so the odd one will not upset a pony.

▼ **Horses enjoy all types of titbits** from carrots and apples to hard mints and treats. Horses have an exceptionally sweet tooth – but never give a horse soft mints as he cannot cope with chewy foods.

peppermint treats

carrots

apples

carrot treats

hard mints

# The horse as a herbivore

Horses are herbivores – they feed only on plants, and are unable to chew or digest meat. Plants do not require hunting or catching as animals do, but are nutritious only in large amounts. So horses must spend a good proportion of their time eating.

## Adapted for grazing

The horse's head shape reveals a great deal about its eating habits. To accommodate the teeth and jaw muscles, the horse has large jaw bones, which is why the head is so long. The eyes are placed well back, allowing the horse to see quite well while he grazes.

There are four types of teeth: canines, incisors, premolars and molars. The last three serve special purposes. The *incisors*, on top and bottom jaws are for cropping food. The first *premolar* on each side is small and not well-developed, but behind it are three more premolars and three *molars*, used for grinding and crushing plant material.

Horses use their big, upper lips to

▼ **Horses** sort through the grass with their sensitive upper lips and crop the juiciest bits with their incisor teeth.

rummage among the herbage. They search for the plants they like best, pushing aside those they don't want.

## Plant digestion

Grass is extremely tough. A horse's teeth are flat, with rough surfaces to crush and grind the cell walls and release the goodness inside.

Horses do not digest their food very efficiently but make up for this with speed. Their rapid digestion makes room for large quantities. It is natural for horses to feed for much of the day, depending on how much food is available and how nutritious it is.

## A balanced diet

As well as grass, horses browse for leaves and other plant material to vary and balance their diets. They sometimes eat thistles, holly and gorse, but take care not to injure their lips. They love fruit, acorns (but these are poisonous in large quantities) and leaves from shrubs and low branches of trees. The horse's long neck enables it to reach these.

Wild horses eat leaves in the summer, saving the grass for winter when the trees are bare.

▲ When food is **scarce** ponies forage in the undergrowth to find any morsels.

◄ When there is **snow** on the ground the horse pushes it out of the way with his muzzle or his hooves to reach the grass below.

**DID YOU KNOW?**
Despite being plant eaters, *stallions* have one canine tooth (used by carnivores for tearing meat) each side of the top and bottom jaws. However, these teeth serve no purpose — mares often have fewer than four canines and sometimes none at all.

◄ **Horses eat** a variety of plants to balance their diets. As well as ground plants, their long, flexible necks allow them to reach the leaves of shrubs and trees.

# Hunger and thirst

In the wild, horses and ponies roam over large areas to find food and water. On average they spend 18-20 hours a day browsing, nibbling and drinking. The life they lead may be very different from that of their domestic cousins.

## From wild to domestic

Living in vast territories allows wild ponies to pick up a variety of foodstuffs: herbs and other plants as well as grass. These plants grow on different soils which provide a range of minerals. For domesticated ponies, supplements to their diets are usually necessary because their paddocks may be limited in minerals.

If wild ponies dislike certain plants or

▲ ▼ **Feeding on different plants** enables wild ponies to pick up a selection of minerals. Together with grass, this varied menu helps to make up a balanced diet, keeping the ponies fit and healthy.

cannot find enough to eat they can move freely on to another area. However, this is rarely possible for domesticated animals, as they are often confined to one field.

A pony limited to food that is nutritionally very poor is constantly hungry, and may start eating poisonous plants, rugs, fencing or faeces.

In cold weather all horses need more nutritious food to keep them warm. In this case, wild horses are sometimes at a disadvantage, as food may be scarce.

## Water for life

Water is vital for life. A pony's body consists of about 70% water. He can live for up to a week without food, but only three days without water.

In the wild, a pony may only be able to drink his fill once or twice a day. He usually spends an hour or more drinking, often pausing and moving away from the water and going back two or three times. In winter, he may receive moisture from snow, and all year round he obtains various amounts from the sap of the plants he grazes on. This is why a grazing pony generally drinks less than a stabled pony on dry feeds.

Ideally, a domestic pony should have access to clean, fresh water at all times. An average-weight 14.2-hand pony needs 20-55 litres (5-12 gallons) of water per day, although he may need slightly less if he is on lush grazing.

▲ **In winter,** when lakes and drinking holes may be frozen over, ponies receive moisture from snow.

▲ **Water** is essential for life and domestic horses must have a constant supply. In the wild where water is not always available, a pony may spend up to an hour quenching his thirst.

# Touch and sensation

Sensory nerves, which respond to touch, heat, cold and pain, are scattered throughout the horse's skin. But a horse's sensitivity varies over the different parts of its body, depending on the number of nerves supplied to each area.

## How horses feel

The nose and muzzle are so sensitive that horses can use them much as we use our fingers. Nerves in the highly sensitive whiskers around the muzzle send messages to the brain whenever they come into contact with something. These messages help the horse to judge how far away an object is and whether or not it may be dangerous. Similar hairs surround and protect the eyes.

Horses also have extremely sensitive backs. They can easily detect flies landing on them and, if you run your finger or a brush gently along a horse's spine, it often dips down in reaction to the contact. Indeed, some horses have such sensitive skin that they dip their backs whenever the saddle is put on. This is known as a 'cold back'.

Continual pressure on a sensitive

**STANDING STILL**

A horse's sensitive skin can be helpful in restraining a naughty horse.

You can make a horse stand still for a few moments by pinching a small fold of skin in the middle of the neck.

▼ **Scratching** an itchy area can be difficult for ponies. This Dartmoor pony finds the solution by rubbing himself against a rock.

area tends to dull feeling. For this reason, pulling at the bit deadens the bars of the mouth and can make a horse insensitive and unresponsive.

## Feeling the heat

Nerves in the skin are not only sensitive to touch. They also respond to heat and cold. When the skin is hot, its blood vessels open up to lose heat. More fluid enters the sweat glands to produce extra sweat and so help cool the horse.

In summer, horses also change their coat and the hairs lie flat to prevent a warming layer of air from being trapped between them.

## Out in the cold

In cold weather, the horse's nerve centre responds to produce the opposite effect. The vessels close up and produce less sweat. If the temperature drops even lower, the hairs stand on end, trapping air in the coat and providing a warm, insulating blanket.

In really cold weather, ponies often indulge in a bit of do-it-yourself 'loft insulation'. They roll about in mud so that they become caked in a messy but effective coat that helps prevent heat loss from the surface of the skin!

◄ **The long sensitive whiskers** help horses determine the texture of the pasture when grazing. This Haflinger has been furrowing in the snow for fresh green grass.

▲ **In the heat** of the midday sun, a herd of Mustangs seek shelter in the shade of trees. Horses can suffer from sunburn if they have any fleshmarks (unpigmented skin) on their coat.

**DID YOU KNOW?**
When horses moult in summer, their coats produce a waterproofing oil known as sebum. This protects the coat and helps keep out the rain so the horse stays cool but dry.

◄ **During the winter,** horses usually grow a thick coat to protect them from the low temperatures. In extreme cold, the long hair on these ponies stands on end to trap air and so warm up their bodies.

# Balance and co-ordination

From the first few minutes of a foal's life, when he tries to stand on his long, spindly legs, balance and co-ordination are vital to his survival.

## Balancing act

When he attempts to get up, the foal draws his feet underneath him and pushes upward. His legs act as a framework that holds his body-weight, with the centre of gravity being a point in the middle of his body. If he moves, his centre of gravity changes and he must then move his legs to even out his weight. If he fails to do this in time, he overbalances.

▼ A new-born foal tries to stand on his long legs. He must find his balance before he is steady on his feet.

At first the foal moves one set of muscles at a time, so each leg acts independently. Muscle co-ordination has to be learned by trial and error, as he obeys the urge to stand.

To allow the foal to be in control of his body movements, his muscles supply him with information. For example, if he moves a limb he can sense its movement. This is because when muscles contract, messages pass to the brain. The other senses also help: the foal can see what is around him, and when his skin comes into contact with something he feels it.

## First steps

Walking presents the foal with a new problem. With each step, one foot must be raised from the ground, so the four-legged frame becomes a tripod. To keep the centre of gravity inside the tripod, the foal has to shift his weight.

When the mare walks leisurely, the foal has to canter to keep up with her. In the wild the foal canters before he can trot. The sequence of steps is the same as in walk, but the rhythm changes and for an instant all four feet are off the ground. Cantering calls for better balance and co-ordination than walking and there is a clear change as the animal moves from one gait to the other.

When the foal is two weeks old he is fully mobile, having mastered the remaining two gaits, the trot and the gallop. These involve different sequences of steps. In the trot the legs must be moved in pairs – left forefoot and right hindfoot, right forefoot and left hindfoot – and this calls for a higher degree of co-ordination. The gallop, which is almost a series of leaps, requires a good sense of balance and judgement.

## Inside the ear

Sensitive instruments deep within the ear tell the foal the position of his body and the way he is moving.

The first instrument consists of two small chambers in each ear. They are lined with sensitive cells and each cell has a hair-like projection.

Tiny loose crystals move freely around the chambers under the influence of gravity. When the foal moves, the crystals move against the hair-like projections, and messages are sent to the brain with information about the foal's position.

The second instrument consists of three

## Advanced steps

When the horse is older, he may have to learn to carry a rider and this affects his balance. The new centre of gravity of horse plus rider is directly above the horse's own centre of gravity. When you ride you help the balance by shifting your weight when necessary, so it stays inside the framework of the legs.

Horses jump over obstacles naturally. As he jumps the horse tucks his legs underneath him, lands on his forelegs and rocks forward as he brings his hindfeet to the ground. He is perfectly balanced the whole time.

Dressage involves exaggerated movements that are based mainly on the horse's natural gaits, but also includes manoeuvres the horse would never do naturally. For example, the half-pass involves moving sideways, crossing the legs over as he does so, leaning his weight over to one side, and moving the outside leg across to restore his balance. This calls for great skill and a trust between the horse and rider.

▲ **Jumping** is a balancing act in which the horse must constantly shift his weight.

► **Dressage** involves complicated moves, so the horse must have excellent balance and co-ordination.

▼ **A horse** with good balance can lean at sharp angles.

semi-circular canals. Two of the canals stand vertically, but at right angles to each other, and the third is horizontal. When the fluid in the canals moves, tiny hairs detect this movement. The three canals then send messages to the brain telling it that the head is moving and what direction it is moving in.

The foal does not have to learn how to use this sensory equipment — it is all automatic. And so are some of the responses to urgent messages: if the foal feels himself overbalancing, for example, he automatically moves to regain his balance.

# Intelligence and survival

Although scientists have developed many different tests for judging an animal's intelligence, the most important measure is how well that animal can survive in its own environment.

## Intelligence tests

The most popular way of testing intelligence involves using food as bait. If an animal presses down on a lever or finds its way through a maze, for example, it gets a titbit. Scientists wait to see how long it takes the animal to find its 'reward' and whether or not it remembers the solution another time.

Generally, horses do not do well when faced with these kinds of test. There is a sad, true story about a herd of wild mustangs in America. The horses always used one particular watering hole. When a short fence was put up across their path, the mustangs only had to walk a few metres along the fence to get past. But the horses could not work this out and, before anyone had realized how bad the situation was, they had all died of thirst. As an illustration of intelligence, this tragedy suggests that horses and ponies are quite stupid – but is this really the case?

## Natural demands

The whole psychology of the horse is based on its physical design. It has no natural defences (like sharp teeth or claws) and so is easy prey to meat-eating animals – unless it can run away. But, as a herbivore, it must spend most of the time with its head down, grazing. So how can it keep a look out for trouble? The answer is to stay with a herd. That way, one or two can be watching while the others graze.

By nature, then, horses are happiest in company with others. They are not

▼ **Buckets usually mean food.** People who look after ponies know that they can learn new routines quite quickly. A pony soon understands the comings and goings of a yard, especially when it's meal-time!

▼ **In a natural environment** horses need to find food and water to survive. They also feel safer living in a herd.

adapted to living on their own. As a group, they can decide when to look for fresh pastures, where to find water, and whether or not a danger is looming. And they do all these things successfully.

## Our involvement

Given horses' natural needs, they have adapted to living with us surprisingly well. Often they live in completely artificial conditions (stables) and must do completely pointless tasks like jumping over fences even though there is no food the other side! They have to gallop hard, without anything chasing them, pull carriages, perform dressage movements and herd cattle.

Although most horses may not be as cunning as their hunters, they have certainly learnt to thrive in partnership with man – and to survive in the wild. In this sense, they show intelligence of the best kind.

◄ **Horses have adapted so well** to our world that they can even help do the difficult job of policing the streets.

▼ **A pony is quick to learn** behaviour which doesn't come naturally to him. This can be as intricate as bowing or as basic as accepting a saddle and bridle.

PART THREE

# HORSE BEHAVIOUR

# Natural behaviour

Certain actions and responses are so deep rooted in the horse that they come to him naturally, even as a new-born foal. Although no one needs to tell him *what* to do, he often has to learn for himself just *how* to do it. This is called innate behaviour and, despite centuries of domestication, it still dictates the way a horse behaves.

## Pregnant mares

In the wild, when a mare is about to foal she moves away from the rest of the herd, looking for somewhere quiet and out of the way to give birth.

If she is disturbed she can delay the birth, for hours if necessary, until she is alone. This behaviour is innate: no other mare has taught her that giving birth is a private matter, she knows it automatically.

After the birth, mother and foal greet each other by touching noses. Then the foal lowers his head and ears, bares his gums and smacks his jaws together. These, too, are innate gestures.

## Finding his feet

The urge to stand comes naturally to the foal and he struggles until he succeeds because he is aware of a new sensation – hunger – and wants to suckle.

◄ **A pregnant mare** knows she wants to be alone in a safe, quiet place when she is about to give birth.

▲ **Soon after birth** the foal feels the urge to stand. He is also beginning to feel hungry.

▲ **Although the foal** is keen to get to his feet, he has to learn just how to steady himself.

▲ **When he is steady** on his feet the foal searches between his mother's legs for her teats. Once he has found them he can satisfy his hunger.

How can the foal know what he feels is hunger and what he has to do about it? He doesn't, but he knows automatically to look for his mother's teats. He searches for two upright structures (his mother's legs) with a dark space between them (the teats). The foal does not realize what it is he is looking for and he may at first make for any dark object – including a nearby human – until he is shown exactly where food is to be found.

Hunger satisfied, the foal must learn to walk. This is something else he must work out for himself, but the desire to walk is innate. As soon as the mare thinks her foal has mastered it she rejoins the herd and the foal follows automatically.

A very young foal follows anything large that moves, believing it to be his mother. This response comes naturally, too. Horses like to be together and when one moves, others follow without thinking about it.

## Out on his own

Soon the young horse starts exploring, sniffing and tasting everything, but he has to learn by trial and error what he can eat and what he can't.

When the youngster meets other horses, he wants to communicate, but like a human child he has to learn by imitation how to communicate correctly.

When a foal sees something strange, fear overcomes curiosity and he flees automatically. Horses are born knowing that when danger threatens they must run. In a risky world, this often helps save their lives.

**Overleaf:** Natural behaviour can help save horses' lives. If a mare starts to run, her foal naturally runs to keep up with her.

▼**Running from danger** is a response that comes naturally to horses.

# All about temperament

▶ **Temperament** shows in a pony's *normal* appearance. Good nature can be detected from a calm look in the eyes, an interested expression and pricked ears.

However, ponies have different moods just like humans, and their temperament depends also on how they are handled.

A horse's temperament refers to his nature, mental outlook on life and how he reacts to the world around. Like people, some horses are good natured and easy going while others can be bad tempered.

## Detecting temperament

The horse's appearance and behaviour are good indications of his temperament. An interested look, ears pricked and a calm expression in the eyes suggests a friendly, honest nature, typical of a pony which is carefully handled and kept in good conditions.

Ears back, a mean or frenzied look in the eyes, with the nostrils slightly drawn back and the tail inclined to

▶ **Keeping a pony** in conditions he does not like — for example, in an enclosed area with an enemy, can make the friendliest of animals agitated and even aggressive. Bad temper is evident in this grey pony by the way he has his ears flattened and is drawing back his nostrils.

▶ **Cold-blooded horses** are ideal for heavy work, such as ploughing, because they usually have kind, co-operative temperaments as well as great strength.

But, this is not always the case. Temperament is inherited and, if one of a horse's parents is slightly highly strung, this quality can easily be passed on, making even a cold blood jumpy.

swish about indicates unfriendliness. But, all ponies have moods and it is their *usual* appearance and behaviour which tell us what sort of temperament they have.

## Types of temperament

The term 'fiery' means an animal is alert and readily sparked into action but also often nervous and easily upset. 'Fiery' usually applies to hot-bloods such as Arabs and Thoroughbreds. However, this is not always the case.

Some native-type ponies, cobs and even cold-blooded breeds – usually steady, willing workers – may be 'fiery' and nervous while some hot-bloods are docile and friendly. Temperament in

these cases is a matter of parentage and character rather than breed alone.

Warm-blooded horses, such as Hanoverians and Trakehners, have been specially bred over generations to give them calm, submissive natures. Words such as 'steady' and 'courageous' applied to warm-bloods mean that they are reliable, they accept training readily and try their hardest under pressure.

## Mixed blood

If you mate a fiery, highly strung stallion with a placid mare, the offspring could take after either one or be a blend of both temperaments.

Stallions are generally more of a handful than geldings and mares.

▼ **Hot-bloods**, like this Arab, are usually 'fiery' in temperament. This means they are very alert and readily 'fired' into action. They can also be nervous and easily upset.

# Different in nature

Just like humans, no two horses are exactly alike – even if they have lived as part of the same herd all their lives. Every horse has certain characteristics that set him apart from all others. His personality is made up of a unique blend of those characteristics he has inherited, those he imitates and those he develops through his own experiences.

## Character building

Horses inherit many of their characteristics (both mental and physical) from their parents, and through them from their ancestors further back. Whether a pony is keen or lazy, nervous or bold, fizzy or placid, depends on heredity.

The basic character and temperament a pony is born with are then moulded by his upbringing and surroundings. From birth, a foal is influenced by his mother's attitudes. If she is wary of humans, for instance, it is quite likely that her foal will follow suit and tread carefully when people are around.

A foal also learns from his stable mates, from his handlers and trainers and from you. When you ride your pony, you become his leader and guide. He looks to you for protection and instructions. If you're not scared of pigs, for example, he'll become less afraid of them himself. On the other hand, if another pony is frightened of pigs, your pony may take his cue from him and run a mile, despite all your efforts to stop him reacting in this way.

## Male dominance

In the wild, when a young male reaches sexual maturity he is challenged by the dominant stallion and the loser is forced to leave the herd. How the youngster copes with the stresses of fighting other stallions and surviving on his own depends on his individual character. Some are nervous and afraid to compete while others are strong and eager to assert themselves as the dominant stallion of the herd.

▼ A horse's character is shaped by the way he lives. In domestication he is influenced by his stable mates and the people who look after him.

◄**When you ride your pony** he looks to you for guidance. Build up a trusting relationship with him and teach him to be calm.

▼**Each foal** is influenced by his mother's character and learns to copy her attitudes.

# Watch this space

▲ **Strangers** need to come to an agreement before entering each other's personal space to become well acquainted.

Every horse lives inside an imaginary bubble. This is called his personal space and he allows others to enter it only if they're invited or if they're friends. Wild horses have an area of land to live in as a group, but they defend this space from other herds only if there is too little food and water to supply them all.

## Private bubble

The horse's personal space is quite small. He has more personal space (about 2-3m/6-9ft) where he has blind spots at the front and back, and slightly less personal space where he has a wide field of vision to his right and left.

The horse carries his personal space with him wherever he goes and chooses who can come into it. The bond between mare and foal allows each of them to enter the other's personal space. Friends accept each other at close quarters, too, but a stranger has to be investigated before he is allowed near.

## Space invasion

When strangers meet, they approach one another cautiously until their invisible bubbles touch. Then they stop. To go on without an invitation would be an invas-

▶ **Domestic horses** get to know the boundaries of their new paddock by walking round the edges and forming a mental map of the area.

ion of personal space. They move closer only when they have agreed to identify each other properly.

In the case of a mare and stallion, the approach may be part of courtship. If the stallion's advances are acceptable, he is allowed to enter the mare's personal space for mating.

Otherwise, horses prefer to keep a little distance between one another. When a horse's space is invaded, he feels threatened. He may move away, or try to drive off the intruder, as happens when a foal comes too close to a mare who is not his mother.

## Home on the range

On a larger scale, a herd of wild horses lives on a *range* of land that provides them with food and water. The horses never mark the boundaries of their range, but know exactly where they lie.

Their range may overlap with that of a neighbouring herd. If the region is rich in resources and the two herds meet, the stallions are unlikely to defend the land itself, but will be far more anxious to keep the invading rivals from stealing any of their valuable mares.

If, however, resources in the region are scarce and enough to support only one herd, the usually peace-loving horses may become *territorial* – the land is no longer just their range, but has become a territory that they will fight hard to defend. When the two herds meet, their stallions, or occasionally their senior mares, do battle. As with other territorial animals, it is usually the defenders of the territory that win. But if the invaders prove victorious, they then become the rightful owners.

## A new home

When a domesticated horse is turned out into a new paddock he often walks all round its edges. He does this to build up a mental map of his new range. Once the map is complete, the horse settles down contentedly and may feel no wish to leave, even when a gate is left open or fences are down.

Perhaps because of stress, a domestic horse may become territorial. Care should always be taken when introducing a new horse to a paddock that is already occupied. If the existing. occupant regards himself as the owner, he may become aggressive and try to drive away the intruder.

▼ **Animals** that fight to defend their home are called territorial, and their home is their territory. In the wild, horses become territorial only when there is not enough food and water for others to share.

# Friendship

▲ **Mutual grooming** helps remove dirt and parasites from the coat. But it also has a social function – it strengthens the bonds of friendship.

Within the herd, individual horses are bound together by personal relationships – they have family and friends. Companionship is extremely important to horses. They are social animals, and a horse kept by himself soon feels very lonely and anxious.

## Playmates

Wild foals start to make friends as soon as they are old enough to play. They need playmates for the chasing and fighting games they enjoy. Close friendships soon develop, but they rarely last. The friends fall out, quarrel, or simply lose interest in one another, just as they would if they were human children.

As they grow older, the colts and the fillies play in separate groups – the colts play much rougher games than the fillies – and so friends are usually of the same sex. Young horses have friends of their own age, so foals make friends with other foals, and yearlings with other yearlings.

## Best friends

Eventually, when they are almost adult, the friendships horses make may last for the rest of their lives. Mares make friends with other mares, and stallions also have favourite mares.

Friends spend as much time together as they can. They stand side by side to shelter from the rain or summer heat. They graze together, often with their heads almost touching.

They also groom each other, working all the way from the neck to the top of the tail. This removes any insects and patches of hard, dried mud that scratching, rubbing or rolling can't always deal with properly.

Often one of a pair seems to be the leader – literally, not in the sense of being the 'boss'! All horses tend to follow other horses, a habit that begins when they are just a few hours old and must learn to stay close to their mothers. Some horses are more curious than others, so they are the first to explore new surroundings – and the others

NEWTON LE WILLOWS
LIBRARY
TEL.01744 677885/86/87

▲ **Horses are happiest** when they are with their friends.

◄ ▼ **The next best thing!** Horses prefer the company of other horses, but can become attached to donkeys and goats if this is not possible.

simply follow them.

Some horses are better than others at making friends. Every horse has its own personality, and often it is much like that of its mother. A timid mare, who does not mix much with others, is quite likely to bring up her foal to be timid.

## Other species

The need for friends is so great that a horse kept by itself befriends other animals if it can. Donkeys and horses often become firm friends, and horses have been known to make friends with goats, dogs, and many other species.

Friendships between horses and humans can become very close. This friendship is not easy to establish – horses are naturally wary of humans, as they are wary of all large, moving objects that might harm them. The human must try to understand the horse's 'language' and see the world from its standpoint. Eventually, if all goes well, the horse comes to treat the human as a kind of 'honorary horse'.

# Body language

Humans rely so much on the voice that body language tends to be overlooked – even among our own kind – as an effective means of communicating. But one of the main ways horses and ponies 'speak' to each other is through their body movements – they let their actions do the talking.

★ **HORSE TALK**
Horses reinforce their body language with sounds – and each noise indicates a different state of mind.
□ **A soft nicker** is usually a sign of welcome or affection.
□ **Whinneys and neighs** tend to convey excitement, pleasure or anticipation.
□ **Squeals** are often a sign of protest – after a painful nip, for example.
□ **Screams** are rare in horses. But the sound of a wild stallion's scream to a rival can be positively spine-chilling!

## Expressing feelings

Horses use every part of their bodies to express themselves. Whether it's the flick of an ear, a look in the eye or a swish of the tail, they communicate with each other just as people do.

**The ears** are extremely expressive. Generally, ears back mean aggression/ threat or extreme effort such as at the end of a race; ears forward mean interest/alertness. Floppy ears are a sign of doziness or feeling unwell.

**The back legs** are a strong, protective and aggressive feature – equivalent to the horns of a bull.

**The front legs** also strike out, often just as a warning, but sometimes 'for real'.

A leg raised in readiness for contact signals to any animals or people nearby that they should keep their distance.

**The tail** can be used almost like a flag in semaphore. Clamped down between the back legs it usually indicates tension. Raised high, the tail shows alertness and well-being. Loosely drooped it means doziness or illness. A tail thrashing about signifies irritation or anger, while some horses or ponies with Arab blood bend their tails back over their quarters in extreme excitement.

## From words to sentences

All of these different signals are used together, helping to convey the true mood of a horse. A combination of head high, ears pricked and tail up means alertness and feeling good; ears floppy, tail down and head low mean tiredness or sickness.

Each sign is like a separate word which, when used with others, makes a complete sentence.

## Horses and humans

The signs a horse uses can be compared to our own actions. A shaken human fist and an outstretched equine head, both accompanied by an angry facial expression, tell the same story! A proud swagger, and conversely a cowering, timid posture or a hunched-up, back-to-the-wind pose, carry the same message in horse and human alike.

## Showing aggression

The horse above has seen something which annoys him. His tail is up, ears back, head thrust forward and he looks cross (**A**). He thrashes his tail in irritation and starts to move (**B**).

In the next stage, he charges toward the rival with his mouth open ready to bite, still looking angry (**C**). When he reaches his rival he decides to back down a bit! He simply threatens by striking out with a foreleg in warning, instead of actually biting (**D**).

# How horses play

▲ **Here a self-confident horse** is simply playing for the sake of it, he's not trying to impress. He leaps and bucks in a straightforward way – just enjoying the sense of freedom. Ears, head and tail are all up and together they indicate liveliness.

▼ **This mare** is using dainty, twisting body movements which seem to be more common in mares than in male horses. She lets herself go and enjoys her playful games. In mixed groups, however, this kind of 'showing off' can be used to confirm status in the hierarchy of a herd.

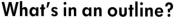

▲ **An alert, startled horse** has its ears pricked, head raised, eyes wide, tail up and is tense.
▼ **A dozing or sick horse** has its ears flopped to the side, eyes half closed, head lowered and one leg resting.

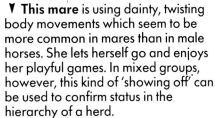

# Striking out in defence

When threatened from behind a horse turns his head so that one eye focuses on the aggressor. His ears go back in annoyance. Defensively, he presents his quarters to warn that he *might* kick (**A**), but the tail clamped protectively down shows that he does not intend to go that far.

He shows a foot, and raises his tail ready to kick as the aggressor is still there (**B**). His ears are back because he is paying attention to what's happening behind him.

To show he means business he lets both his hindlegs fly back (**C**), with ears still back and tail well up, thrashing in anger. His rival swerves away in self-defence.

# Telling a horse's mood

You can usually tell a horse's mood by the position of his ears, eyes and muzzle. Studying the different facial expressions helps you to interpret what a horse is thinking and to discover whether or not he is happy.

## Look at the ears

The most valuable indicator of a horse's mood is his ears. Horses tend to point their ears in the direction of their concentration. They seem to 'look' with their ears.

For instance, if you are cantering toward a jump and your horse's ears are pricked toward it, he will probably jump clear. But if his ears are back, it's quite likely that he will either knock it down or run out. If he's worried about the jump he may point his ears forward, but also tense up and either rush at the fence or refuse it.

Try to get into the habit of watching horses, whatever they are doing, so that you can learn to read their minds. Once you recognize the signs, you'll see just how expressive horses' faces really are. In no time at all, understanding horses' moods becomes second nature.

**! TALKING NOSES**
Many horses have expressive nostrils. Aroused horses tend to flare their nostrils. This can be when they are playing or when they are afraid or startled.

A wrinkled nose, on the other hand, is a sign of annoyance so beware! A horse wrinkles his nose as a mild threat and also when he's in pain or irritated.

▲ **Contentment:** While a horse feels relaxed and satisfied his top lip may look longer than usual and come over the bottom lip. His ears are a little limp and floppy and tend to droop to the sides. The eyes are soft with a dreamy look.

▲ **Fear:** The ears are probably back, especially when the pony is scared of something behind him, or of the rider. His eyes are wide open and his nostrils become flared. The whites of the eyes may show, if the pony rolls them in an effort to see what is frightening him.

▲ **Threat:** The ears are flattened back, the nostrils wrinkle up and back. The horse's face looks angry and his mouth is open, sometimes with the teeth showing. It's important to recognize this expression so that you don't get bitten!

▲ **Attention:** When a horse concentrates, investigates something or meets another horse, his ears are usually pricked forward. The nostrils flare a little and the top lip may quiver as the pony 'feels' and smells the object of interest.

▲ **Disgust:** Similar to a threatening look, the horse's ears are half back, his nostrils wrinkle up and back and he has a rather cross look of distaste about him. Unlike a threat, the mouth is not open but the top lip sometimes curls up and back.

## ❗ RECOGNIZING STRESS

The horse's *muscles* also help you to understand his feelings. When frightened or excited the muscles become tense and hard.

You can tell whether a horse is stiff or trembling by stroking his neck. If he feels stressed, walk him round and reassure him with soothing pats to calm him down.

When he's relaxed, the muscles are softer and, unless he's shivering from the cold, he does not tremble.

▲ **Dozy:** If a horse dozes, his ears tend to flop to the sides, his head lowers, his bottom lip may sag a little and his eyes half close. When he actually falls asleep his eyes close completely, his head lowers even more and the bottom lip drops further.

▲ **Yawning:** Ponies yawn if they are bored, tired or short of fresh air — for just the same reasons as we do. The head goes up, the ears go forward and, like us, the mouth opens wide with the lips back showing the teeth. The eyes are at least half closed.

## ★ EAR TALK

Ears pointing backward are not *always* a sign of bad temper or fear. When a horse is listening to what's going on behind him, he will put his ears back.

Sometimes a horse's ears point in different directions. This usually means that he's listening to two sounds at the same time.

# Horse talk

The horse's main means of communicating is to let his actions do the talking. But sounds are important, too: whether it's a whinny, a whicker, a squeal or a scream, the horse is saying something to those in the know.

### Friendly intentions

The most familiar sound a horse makes is the neigh. Loud and high pitched, it is also versatile: a horse neighs to a friend in the distance or to check if there are any other horses close by; mares do it to find a missing foal; and an outdoor horse greets a human arriving at his field in this way.

Other friendly noises are the whinny, which is a soft, quiet neigh, and the whicker (or nicker), which is low pitched and soft. Horses use them to show affection to friends and members of their family and to people that they are fond of and have grown to trust.

A whinny might also mean the pony is on the lookout for a tasty titbit, while a whicker is like a sigh of relief when it finally turns up.

### Alarm signals

Less friendly are noises such as squeals and screams. Signalling displeasure or aggression, a short, faint squeal is likely to be accompanied by ears back and nostrils wrinkled. A bite could well be on the way!

Just as ominous, but much louder and more high pitched is a scream. Two rival stallions will confront each other with this spine-chilling noise, along with much shaking of the head and mane, and general stamping of the ground – all signs of warning and aggression.

### Courting calls

A mixture of squeals, whinnies and snorts probably means there is courtship in the air. The stallion snorts and whinnies as he woos his mare. She responds to his calls with the odd squeal and appealing whicker.

▼ **When they are re-united** with their friends, horses often make a gentle whickering noise in their throats to express their pleasure.

►**As frightening as the body language** of rival stallions are the spine-chilling screams they give to ward each other off.

## How sounds are made

The larynx (voicebox) is attached to the trachea (windpipe). It has two flexible tissues (the vocal cords) stretched across it. Normally they are apart, but when a noise is required the vocal cords are brought together by muscles. As the horse forces air between the cords in an attempt to make a sound, they vibrate and produce a noise.

The same happens when you hold a blade of grass or a privet leaf between your thumbs and blow. The tighter you stretch the leaf, the faster the vibrations are and the more high pitched the noise that is produced. The horse's vocal cords work in just the same way — the horse knows how tight to stretch them to make just the noise he wants.

Horses who develop breathing problems often need an operation on their larynx that leaves them unable to make a noise. The only means of communication left to these horses is body language.

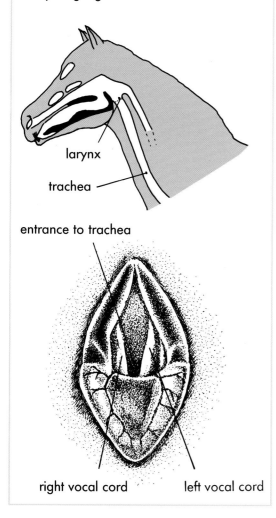

larynx

trachea

entrance to trachea

right vocal cord          left vocal cord

**Sounds are very important to horses.** Friends learn to recognize each other as much by their voices as by their physical appearance.

# The importance of play

**! FOAL CHECK**
Weaning foals too early can be a setback for them. Lack of a mother's supervision can lead to bad manners. This can be overcome by putting a 'nanny' (a non-milking mare) or a gelding with the youngsters to set an example and keep them in check.

Playing is a way for youngsters to learn how to communicate with each other, preparing them for adult life. It also helps to develop their bodies and teaches them their place within the herd.

## Play from birth

Everything is new to a foal and has to be investigated. He begins playing with his mother, or on his own. First, he learns to co-ordinate his long legs and to stabilize himself. He does this by experimenting with walking and trotting, while frolicking. He may put his head down and give a little buck, or toss his head and prance before cantering, as he grows older.

The foal may nibble his mother, tug at her mane and tail, charge at her, bump into her and even nip at her legs as she walks. When the mare lies down, the foal may climb on her, paw her with his hooves, nibble her and sometimes even sit on top of her! These playful actions strengthen the bond between a foal and his mother.

## Communication

Young foals stay near their mothers – the close relationship is essential for survival. The dam teaches the foal 'herd manners' and 'horse language' for communicating with others. This helps him to be accepted by members of the herd.

Hand-reared foals, brought up by humans instead of by their mother, often don't know how to communicate properly with other horses. As a result, they may be bullied or 'cast out'.

## Growth and development

As play strengthens the young horse's body and teaches him co-ordination, he is able to join in confidently with others.

At first they approach each other, with their heads up and ears pricked

**▼ ► While frolicking** the foal learns to stabilize himself on his long legs, and practises trotting and cantering. He plays with his mother at first, or by himself, for exercise and fun.

and may sniff each other. Sometimes they squeal, toss their heads and strike out with their forelegs. This may lead to mutual grooming.

Foals can often be seen prancing alongside each other, play-bucking, kicking and rearing, waving their front legs and trying to grab each others' crests with their teeth.

One foal may try to get his legs over another's neck and it seems that the one who succeeds is 'top dog'. This jostling for position is how foals learn who is strongest and where they stand within the herd society. Those who are mentally and physically strongest – and not necessarily the biggest – gain the highest social positions.

▼ **Play** becomes more vigorous as the foal grows stronger. Here a youngster gives a little buck as a playful warning to another foal.

► **Mutual grooming** is part of the play-process. Youngsters learn to communicate with each other, forming bonds of friendship.

**▲ Youngsters**
sometimes play-mount
as a result of seeing
adults mating. Colts,
when they are
sexually mature, can
even get females in
foal.

when in season, and even get them in
foal. Colts see adults mating and copy
stallions mounting mares.

Yearling colts play boisterously, rearing, striking out with their forefeet,
biting and becoming quite aggressive.
This is preparation for the battles between rival males for the leadership of a
herd.

Fillies are gentler with each other and
use the same play patterns as when they
were younger – prancing, galloping, head
tossing, bucking, pretend kicking, nipping at each other and mutual grooming, with no rearing and striking out.
These patterns continue for life.

## Herd formation

By the time they are yearlings, the
youngsters have learned their position
in the herd, although this changes as
other members become old or sick, or for
some reason leave the herd.

In the wild, females usually remain in
a group and form very strong family
bonds, though one or two may be
abducted by an outside stallion to form a
new herd. When females have foals of
their own, they often become aggressively protective and teach them the play

By the time they are 12 months old,
young horses, now called yearlings, are
quite independent of their dams.

## Colts and fillies

In domesticated studs, yearlings are
usually separated into colt and filly
groups as they become sexually mature.
Stallion instincts surface in the colts:
they can harass fillies and older females

**► Play** can be quite
aggressive in colts.
They prepare for the
rivalry they are likely
to face as adult
stallions.

► **Females** are more gentle at play than colts. They may gallop and prance around, but there is little or no play-fighting in their games.

and behaviour patterns they learned from their own dams.

Males are chased out of the herd by the reigning stallion when they become sexually mature, as they are a threat to his position as leader. The defeated males live alone or form bachelor bands.

## Play time

Most horses, wild or domesticated, like to play no matter what their age. In a stable, a horse looks for entertainment such as prising off kicking boards, lifting his manger or bucket out of its holder and maybe throwing it around the stable. He may chew anything left within reach such as a headcollar or rug and, if cooped up for too long, may develop vices.

To combat this, all horses should ideally be given time every day to play freely outside, preferably with other horses, so they can let off steam and exercise themselves.

▼ **Kicking out** is another boisterous action seen during play between colts. As stallions, this striking out with the forefeet becomes vicious rearing.

► **Males** are forced to leave a herd by the dominant stallion, when they are mature enough to mate. Lone stallions and colts sometimes live singly, but more often stay together in 'bachelor' groups, until they form herds of their own.

## HORSE PLAY

To keep a stabled pony amused try giving him something to play with. A plastic football in a hay net, half a car tyre suspended with baler twine in a corner, or a plastic bottle filled with water and suspended in the same way, are all safe and successful toys for horses.

# Time for a roll

★ **THE SHAKES**
A pony that rolls continually without shaking off the dust when he gets up may be in pain. Colicky ponies try to roll away their internal discomfort and only succeed in making themselves worse.

▼**Ponies appreciate** a roll after exercise. If you want to let your tired pony roll in some shallow water after a ride, it's a good idea to safeguard his valuable saddle by removing it before he collapses in a heap.

It's hard for humans to understand why ponies like rolling so much. Their other pastimes, such as eating, sleeping and drinking have an obvious function and people enjoy them, too. Rolling has a charm all of its own for ponies, but they must learn that there is a time and a place for everything. A pony must never roll when at work.

## What's the attraction?

Horses and ponies roll for a variety of reasons. Wild or feral horses roll to establish herd unity: relatives roll in one place, which takes on their family scent. Domesticated ponies often roll one by one on the same patch of ground for the same purpose of creating a family feeling.

Rolling in dry earth helps keep a pony's coat clean. Fine dust presses into his coat and absorbs excess grease. When they have been shampooed, many ponies feel uncomfortable and want a roll to help them dry off. Rolling also discourages parasites and relieves inaccessible itches and sweat patches after exercise – very comforting for a pony.

Rolling in mud is fine. Dried mud on his coat does the field-kept pony no harm provided he is not allowed to get wet.

Ponies often enjoy rolling just for the fun of it. Soft sand, cold streams on a hot day or sticky mud can all make horses go down with a grunt of pleasure.

A few ponies roll simply to dislodge their riders. If they are feeling fed up, they may lie down and refuse to move, but this is very rare.

## Roll over and relax

Stable-kept ponies must be allowed the opportunity to roll in an open space after exercise. If they aren't, they may have a go in a confined space and become cast (stuck) or injure themselves. A pony that has become cast may be disturbed by this experience, and be reluctant to lie down again when he's indoors.

An exercise paddock or playpen is the best place to turn out a pony so he can roll before he goes in. Outdoor manège or indoor school surfaces are good places for rolling, since the materials that go to make them up, such as shavings and sand, brush off easily. ➤

**Pawing** is a sign that a pony is thinking of a pleasant roll. If you are riding him at the time, you are in danger of being crushed. Be alert to the signs, especially when riding in water. Keep a contact with the reins, bring the pony's head up and make him walk on if he paws.

► **Soft mud** may be fun to roll in, but if the pony stays out in the rain the mud pack will badly affect his coat's insulation.

 **CAREFUL CONTACT**
A pony that has a reputation for rolling while being ridden is a menace. If you ride such a pony, be sure always to keep a contact, sit up and keep him moving.

▼ **It's good to see** a pony having a roll. Some say that a pony that can roll right over is athletic and well built.

## Dangerous moves

It's extremely dangerous for your pony to roll when he is being ridden or driven. Horses and ponies are heavy, and if one rolls on you, a broken arm, leg, pelvis, rib or back could be the result. At worst, you may suffer internal crush injuries. At best, your valuable saddle might be damaged by the weight of the pony.

A driven pony can bring down a companion, damage the vehicle, get caught in the harness, panic, thrash about and injure himself.

## Be alert to the signs

You must do all you can to prevent a pony rolling when he's at work, so it's essential to be aware of the signs. When they are about to roll, most ponies come to a standstill, lower their heads to inspect the ground or water, then start to paw it. Next, they buckle at the knees and lower the shoulder of the side they want to roll on first, before sinking to the ground.

If your pony seems unduly interested in the ground, let him see it but keep a short enough rein to have some contact with his mouth. Watch him carefully – he may only be reaching down for a drink or some grass.

If he starts to paw (he may not always do this), or you feel his knees bending, bring his head up with repeated jerks on the reins, especially on the side he wants to go down on. Kick him hard to make him move forward – you could even use your whip. This sounds brutal but it is an emergency. Sit up straight – if you lean forward he may pull you over his head –

▼ **A good shake** is the final stage in the rolling routine. The pony gets rid of all the excess sand and dust he has been rubbing into his back and sides.

and command him to walk on. Shout if he doesn't obey you straightaway.

Once he's moving, keep a contact and avoid the spot he favours for rolling – he may be tempted to try again.

### *Bail out*

If you don't manage to prevent the pony's forehand going down, then it's too late to try to get him up. It's time to dismount quickly – quit your stirrups at once and step off on the downward side (the side he's going down on). This means you are out of the way of his thrashing legs.

If you are driving and your pony seems intent on rolling, jerk up the reins, use the whip and shout. If this doesn't work,

abandon the carriage immediately as an accident could follow.

Get hold of his head as quickly as possible and urge him to get up – this can be difficult if he's enjoying himself. Try to hang on to the reins to prevent them getting entangled in his legs, but don't endanger yourself.

While the pony is rolling against your will, scold him – he must understand the difference between rolling during work and rolling off duty. Don't hit him, though, as he may try to get up in a panic and hurt himself. Once he has finished, don't punish him – he won't know what on earth he's done wrong and will be confused and hurt by your anger.

**Overleaf:** Riding in water is fun for you and your pony and a great way to cool down. Just be sure you are ready to stop your pony rolling in the inviting water and taking you and your saddle with him.

## Going down

◣ **This gleaming stallion** hits the deck for a long, sandy roll on a hot summer's day. Soft sand is high on the list of preferred rolling surfaces for horses.

►**If you bath your pony** before a show make sure he can't get loose and roll while he's still wet. A freshly shampooed horse can't wait to get down and roll away that uncomfortable squeaky-clean feeling.

95

# Homing instincts

**▼ Horses** build mental maps of their surroundings, whether they live wild, in wide open spaces, or within the boundaries of a field (inset).

If you become separated from your friends in unfamiliar countryside and lose your way, sit tight and let the horse go where he wishes. There is a good chance he'll find his own way home.

## Sense of direction

Horses are very observant. They use their observations to build a mental map of their surroundings.

When a horse is turned out into a new field, one of the first things he usually does is walk all around the edge. Once he has done this, and knows the boundaries, he is quite content. The horse may not bother to explore farther even if the gate is left open.

Wild horses cover large distances, but

they too recognize boundaries and know where they are. The range in which they live is often large and they are not interested in moving outside it, unless they are compelled to leave in search of food and water. Within the range they soon learn all the landmarks and can find their way quickly and easily from one place to another.

Horses use their 'maps' every day of their lives, because they like particular places to eat, sleep and rest. These places are all chosen for different reasons. For example, a rest spot should be sheltered, with a good all-round view and protection from insects, while an eating area has the juiciest grass!

## Navigation by smell

A horse has a keen sense of smell, which it uses to map out certain landmarks. If you watch a horse finding its way in strange country, it stops to sniff around wherever the track divides. A horse may be searching out the smell of its own hoofprints to tell where it has already been, or seeking scents remembered from earlier travels.

There is no firm explanation of this, but the path the horse chooses often turns out to be the right one.

## Homing magnet

Apart from sight and smell, some animals – and the horse is believed to be one of them – carry 'magnetic compasses' in their heads. Haemoglobin, which gives blood its red colour, is rich in iron. Iron becomes concentrated to make a mineral known as magnetite in a part of the brain.

The 'homing' pigeon is the best example of an animal using this mineral 'compass' to orientate itself in relation to the earth's magnetic field.

It is important for horses to be able to find their way around in the wild. And from your point of view, it's useful to ride an animal whose combination of eyes, ears and mind can take you unerringly home when you are unsure of the way yourself!

▲ **Horses can often find their way home,** using a mixture of sight, smell and intuition.

▼ **Smell is a useful guide,** when searching for water in dry country. It is vital for a wild horse to find its way around.

# Natural grooming

The skin, with its protective barrier of hair, is one of the horse's most important organs. Grooming – performed by the horses themselves in the wild – is vital to maintain its healthy condition.

### Skin care

Apart from encasing the internal organs, the skin plays several roles in the horse's well being.

First, it helps to regulate the horse's body temperature. The coat traps a thin layer of warm air next to the skin when it's cold, and a cool breeze blows through the hairs in hot weather. But caked mud and a clogged-up coat stop this insulation working effectively, so it's essential that the dirt is removed, loose hair cleaned away and the individual hairs kept separate.

Grooming also prevents the pores from blocking, for the second task of the skin is to release waste products. At the same time, getting rid of parasites and mud stops harmful substances *entering* through the skin: insect bites can transmit disease and wounds must be cleaned so dirt can't seep in and cause infection.

Finally, the skin provides the pony with information about the outside world. It has a rich supply of nerve endings which detect pain, temperature or touch, and these are sharpened by the stimulating massage of grooming.

### Grooming patterns

A healthy horse grooms himself whenever he feels discomfort which, in the wild, can be many times a day. If an itch needs to be scratched it may lead to a

▼ **The mutual grooming ritual** between horses helps to strengthen their bonds of friendship and trust.

full grooming session, which makes the horse feel comfortable and relaxes him if he is anxious.

The principal tools are the tongue and incisor teeth for smoothing and nibbling. The long, flexible neck lets the horse reach most of its body with its mouth. Young horses may use a hind hoof to scratch behind their ears, but this gives way to rolling as they grow older.

Once the legs and lower part of the body have been licked and nibbled the horse attends to its neck, shoulders, withers and rump – the parts its mouth cannot reach – by rolling. Horses have their favourite places for rolling, usually somewhere dusty or in water.

Sometimes, while on their feet, horses use rocks, trees or even fence posts to scratch themselves thoroughly.

## Mutual grooming

Horses also groom one another. The ritual begins with an invitation from one horse to another, expressed by wiggling the nose, with the mouth slightly open. If the invitation is accepted the two stand side by side and attend to the withers and sometimes to the tail region as well. These sessions last up to ten minutes.

Because grooming makes the horse feel comfortable, it is a service one friend or relative can give to another that reinforces their friendship. It is also a sign of trust for a horse to allow another animal to come so close. Each horse has only a few grooming partners.

◄ **A foal's flexible neck** allows him to nibble his body with his teeth, to relieve any irritations.

◄ **Itches** in awkward places can be soothed by rubbing against a sturdy object such as a fence rail.

▼ **Rolling** scratches the parts of the body that the horse cannot reach with his mouth, such as his neck.

**For all-round health,** ponies need their skin and coat kept in good condition by grooming.

# Rituals and displays

★ **PART OF THE FAMILY**

If a stallion shows interest in a mare and wants her to be part of his herd, he may perform the ritual of urinating on her dung-pile. In this way, he leaves his scent and demonstrates his superiority.

▼ **Once one horse** has been allowed to enter another's personal space, the two go through the ritual of smelling each other, at first, nose to nose.

A ritual is a form of recognized behaviour. All mammals have rituals, and those of horses are very elaborate. It all starts when two horses meet.

## The encounter

When horses are strangers, they usually approach one another and pause a little way apart. Each one is surrounded by its own 'personal space', and others can only come close when they are invited.

The horses watch each other's facial expressions, ear movements and body postures. These reveal whether they are friendly or hostile. A nursing mare often rejects even friendly approaches to protect her foal.

If the meeting is unwelcome the two horses separate. But if it is friendly they move closer, inside each other's personal space. At this uncertain stage, they stand at a slight angle to keep out of the way of a sudden kick from a foreleg, and they make welcoming or warning sounds. The horses may flick their ears, according to their mood, and then start sniffing each other. Horses communicate by smell.

The sniffing starts 'nose to nose' and proceeds to a thorough investigation of the whole body. By the end of the encounter the two may feel so relaxed and friendly that the greeting leads to a session of mutual grooming.

## Stallion rituals

The meeting of two stallions is rather different. A herd only contains one adult male and an encounter between stallions from different herds becomes a challenge.

Each stallion checks that his herd is

together, out of the way of his rival, so there is no risk of losing any mares. Then he approaches the other stallion.

The meeting could develop into a fight so each male does his best to convince the other that he is the fitter and stronger. He makes his muscles bulge, snorts loudly and takes high, exaggerated, prancing steps. Each stallion holds his head high, with his ears back and generally looks as big and fierce as he possibly can.

The two circle one another, being sure to keep out of range of flying hooves, while they intimidate each other. Often this is enough. One stallion realizes he is out-classed and retreats, taking his mares with him.

## The dunging ritual

If a show of strength does not settle the matter the two males may go through the 'dunging ritual'. While still prancing and posturing one of the stallions finds a pile of dung.

He deposits his own dung on top of the pile, with exaggerated sniffing. His rival then repeats the operation, and the two alternately sniff the pile, deposit dung and sniff again, until one contestant admits his defeat and leaves.

The dunging ritual demonstrates one stallion's superiority: if the scent on top of the pile is his, he is superior.

True fights among wild stallions are rare. The ritual should resolve the contest between them without the risk of injury. However, domestic horses may not have enough space to retreat and a fight may be the result.

◄ **If the initial meeting** between two horses is successful, a session of mutual grooming may follow the sniffing ritual.

▼ **An encounter** between two adult males is a challenge. Here an alert stallion approaches his rival, leaving his herd of mares safely behind him.

# Greeting and courtship

When two horses who don't know each other meet for the first time, they are inquisitive and draw close for inspection. But what is going through their minds during the first encounter?

## First impressions

On meeting a stranger, the horse's immediate sequence of thoughts probably goes something like this.

I can see a large object, the size of a horse. What is it? (Moves a bit closer.) It *is* a horse. Do I know it? (Moves a bit closer.) No, it's a stranger. Is it male or female? (Begins to be cautious.) Does it want to be friends? Yes, it does. (Approaches with a greeting.)

The ritual of meeting and greeting is known as a 'behavioural programme' – this is a set of body movements and sounds that all horses understand.

Unlike the automatic responses to drink when thirsty, or eat when hungry, behavioural programmes are learned, and it is up to the horse to decide how and when to use them. Despite the rituals of social encounters, the outcome of a meeting is not always certain.

## The new arrival

If, when two horses meet in the wild, one of them shows hostility to the other, the encounter ends there and then.

The curiosity domestic horses feel about one another, however, can lead to trouble. If a new horse is led into a field containing a herd, the horses tend to rush forward, all jostling to be first to inspect the new arrival.

The sight of so many strangers bearing down at once can be alarming. The new horse may panic and try to run away, causing a stampede, or hurt himself by trying to escape from the field.

Care is needed when introducing a horse into a herd. The best way is to separate the newcomer from the others with a temporary fence for the first few days. The horses can approach and get to know one another, but the newcomer can escape to safety if he feels the need to get away.

## Courtship

Courtship is a ritual, too, and like any other social encounter between horses, it can be a tricky situation.

When a stallion wants to mate with a mare in season, he arches his neck, tucks

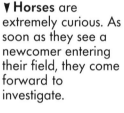
▼ **Horses** are extremely curious. As soon as they see a newcomer entering their field, they come forward to investigate.

▲**During courtship** the stallion's body language informs the mare that he is keen to mate. She also knows that he won't proceed until she gives him the go ahead.

►**Meeting**: When getting to know each other, horses all behave in the same way. They learn this greeting ritual early on in their lives.

in his chin, lifts his tail and performs a high-stepping prancing sort of dance. In spite of this impressive show of his keenness to mate, the stallion's still unsure of himself and frightened of being rejected. The stallion won't enter the mare's 'personal space' – for fear of being kicked – until she is prepared to allow him to approach. If he can persuade her to stand still, he greets her nose to nose, and starts grooming her in the early stages of his mating ritual.

At any time, though, the mare may have second thoughts and move away, and the stallion has to begin his courtship dance all over again. This behaviour is a standard ritual and the stallion may have to repeat it many times before he can successfully mate with the mare.

# The signs of contentment

In general horses are happy when their way of life is similar to that of their wild ancestors: living in a group, in the open air with plenty to see all around. Under these circumstances most horses feel safe and relaxed.

## Contented expressions

Watch the expressions on a horse's face, the position of his ears, his body posture and the way he holds his tail. All of these features indicate the kind of mood he is in.

The horse's overall appearance, when he is at ease, is one of calmness. In fact he often looks fast asleep. His muscles are relaxed, his head and tail are held low and he rests on one hip.

If he is dozy his face is free of tension, with relaxed nostrils, his top lip drooping over the bottom one and his ears

► **Horses and ponies** feel secure when they have plenty of space around them and friends to communicate with.

◄ ▼ **Friendship** is vital for happiness. Horses, like humans, enjoy the company of others.

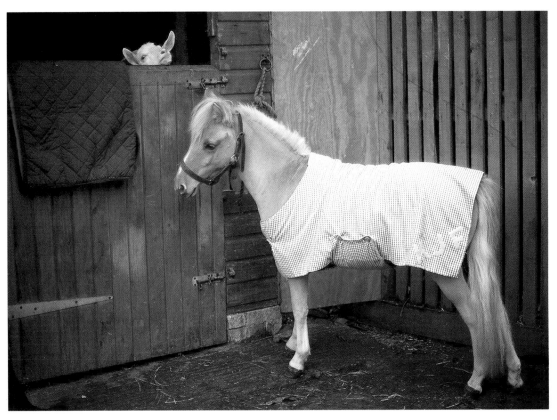

flopping to the sides or slightly backward. His eyes, which may be half closed, have a dreamy expression. Sometimes, if the horse is really relaxed, he may even lean against a convenient wall, tree or fence post.

## The outdoor type

Many animals feel secure in a small, enclosed space where their enemies cannot reach them, but this is not the case for horses. They generally prefer to be in the open, with ample warning of approaching danger and time and space to escape by running.

Although most horses enjoy being outdoors, they need protection from bad weather, especially the wind. The horse needs interesting surroundings to keep him occupied and room to move from one place to another.

## Friendship

The horse is a social animal and the presence of others increases his contentment, whether he is in a field or in his stable.

Although some horses may be perfectly happy when they are on their own, others become nervous, neurotic and depressed. Mixing with others provides friendship, communication, mutual grooming and play among youngsters. If no other horses are nearby then a horse befriends almost any other animal.

It is quite easy to tell whether or not a horse is enjoying life once you learn to read the signs. A contented horse is calm and even tempered. If he is well fed and healthy, he looks it.

The clearest signs of contentment are a relaxed, friendly manner, a gleaming coat and bright, confident eyes.

▲ **A relaxed manner** indicates contentment. Taking a nap is a sure sign that the horse feels at ease.

# Herd behaviour

Horses are social animals. In the wild, they live with their family and friends in closely knit groups. They keep each other company and protect each other from danger.

## Forming groups

Mare groups – which are usually led by a stallion – consist of about 12 horses. Within the group there is a clearly defined pecking order with status depending on age and strength. The lead stallion has complete control and no other horse in his group dares to challenge his authority. Each group also has a senior mare. The other mares and their foals complete the herd.

Stallions without mares, such as young colts and older horses past their prime, find companionship by grouping together. These groups are known as bachelor groups.

## On the move

Herds have regular patterns of movement between morning, afternoon and night.

There are also seasonal movements. For instance, horses may move to a certain part of the range searching for

▲ **Two rival stallions** challenge each other, fighting for dominance of a water hole in Wyoming.

► **Domestic horses** retain their strong instinct to remain in a herd. But each horse prefers to have its own distance of at least 1 m (3ft) in front and behind.

grass in late autumn, and another area in early spring when the new grass comes through.

Movement is not necessarily initiated by the leader. A dominant mare often goes first and the others follow. The stallion acts as a herdsman, making sure no horse strays and protecting the group from danger.

If another herd approaches, the stallion always goes ahead of the group to challenge the rival leader. Fights between neighbouring stallions are quite common but seldom cause a bad injury.

Stallions attack with their forefeet, rearing up and striking out viciously at the rival. They also kick out with their hindfeet and sometimes bite.

## Keeping their distance

Just as different groups keep their distance from one another, so do the individuals within each group.

When grazing, horses like to keep several metres apart from one another. This gives them room to move quickly if they are startled by something from behind. If a horse or foal accidentally enters the territory of another, a horse often strikes out in defence.

▲ **A foal** rarely strays far from its mother. Even when grazing, the mare keeps a constant guard over her offspring, listening or watching to make sure it is safe and sound.

★ **NATURAL INSTINCTS**
In show-jumping competitions, horses sometimes 'nap' or try to return to the collecting ring where the other horses are waiting.

They want to return to the collecting ring because horses, as herd animals, have a natural instinct to return to or remain with their own kind.

# Groups of horses

▲ **When introducing** a pony into a group, give the established horses time to get to know and accept the newcomer. Never simply bundle a new pony straight into a herd of strangers.

If there *are* personality clashes, remember it *could* be your pony that's at fault, so be prepared to accept it with good grace. If he obviously is the bully, you'll need to separate him from his enemy.

Keeping several ponies together in a large field is the nearest most owners can get to nature – where wild horses live in herds with space to graze and move, to escape from predators or other unfriendly horses, and to seek shelter.

## The pros and cons

As well as the *ponies* leading more natural lives and forming normal social relationships with others, there are advantages for the owners, too.

You can all share field chores such as picking up droppings, helping with pasture care, mucking out the shelter, and checking fencing and water. Well-cared for grass is a suitable and economical food for much of the year so the owners can save money on feed costs.

However, the horses and their pasture must be properly managed. For ponies living out much of the time, you should allow two acres for the first animal and one for each subsequent animal. This gives the horses a feeling of enough space and allows you to divide the land into at least two paddocks. Anything less than this means the ponies are overcrowded, and eat certain areas of grass down to the ground while ignoring others which they designate as lavatory areas.

As less and less grass is available, the horses become hungry and on edge. Bullying sets in which can result in injuries and in the more timid animals being kept away from shelter, water or hay. The owners have to give extra feed which is expensive and inconvenient.

You must also work out a proper rota with the other owners. Otherwise you may disagree over worming programmes, feeding arrangements and chores.

Your vet will advise on a worming programme. He will probably recommend that you worm every horse and pony – at the same time – every six or eight weeks all year round, depending on the wormer used, the amount of land and the number of animals. It is essential that all the animals *are* wormed together every time, otherwise those not treated simply re-infect the others straight away.

## Character clashes

Like humans, horses form relationships, making friends and enemies. Some are 'top dogs', some are 'bottom of the ▶

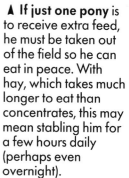

▲ **If just one pony** is to receive extra feed, he must be taken out of the field so he can eat in peace. With hay, which takes much longer to eat than concentrates, this may mean stabling him for a few hours daily (perhaps even overnight).

When feeding hay in the field, provide one extra hay net — this helps to avoid bullying.

◄ **Ponies enjoy company** and prefer to be kept in groups. Like humans, they make particular friends and may 'pair off' to graze.

◄ **When you want to catch** only one pony, make sure you don't let the others out! Open the gate just wide enough for you both to walk out, then shut it quickly — but don't bang your pony's quarters in the process.

heap' and others are in between. Normally, there is little bullying when horses feel well-fed, healthy and have plenty of space. However, if serious personality clashes still occur, you've no choice but to separate the offenders by grazing them in different paddocks or at different times.

Problems can also arise when some ponies need feeding but others don't. It is not practical to feed some and not others as jealousy and fights occur and food is stolen. Those needing extra feed should be brought out of the field while they eat their ration (about 10–20 minutes), then returned.

When you want to take just one pony out for feeding or work, adopt a confident attitude, particularly if you are expecting the others to mill round and hustle you. Speak sharply and push them away, hard. Most ponies respect your wishes – but you may need a friend's help with the difficult ones.

Leaving a well-fitting headcollar on your own pony makes him easier to catch in a throng. At the gate, push, or even smack, the others as far away as you can and open the gate just wide enough to get your pony through but without risking his knocking himself. A catching pen is a great help. Most herds, however, become used to individuals being taken away and returned at varying times, and cause no problems.

## Introducing a new pony

Introducing a pony into an established herd can cause trouble. He is regarded as an intruder and may well be on the receiving end of nasty kicks and bites until his position in the herd hierarchy – the 'pecking order' – is established.

Avoid this by turning him out (and so making friends) with just one herd member at first, usually one of the lower ranking ones. You will need two paddocks, or divide one in two sections.

Over a few days, if possible, gradually introduce the other ponies back in, one by one, the highest-ranking members last. This way, the newcomer does not feel strange and the returning herd members see that he has been accepted and has acquired some confidence.

►**Ponies**, particularly hardy native breeds, relish the freedom of a large field all year round. Allow two acres for the first horse and one for each pony after that.

# Dominance and leadership

Most wild herds consist of several mares, their young, and a stallion – in fact a family. The stallion is superior to all other males, but not to the mares!

### The challenge

A stallion tries to drive out any other male who threatens his position. Even his sons, when sexually mature, have to leave the herd. He challenges any stallion that might steal one of his 'wives'.

His success in these contests depends on whether he has the ability to win a fight. Unless the rivals are closely matched, they do not actually fight because the outcome is obvious to both of them and one gives way.

When one individual asserts its authority over another it is said to be 'dominant'. The weaker one is described as 'subordinate'.

Once dominance is established, the animals involved accept it as a matter of course. When they meet, the subordinate horse moves out of the way of the dominant one, perhaps making a submissive gesture as it does so. These relationships provide the basis of 'dominance hierarchies'.

### Fighting force

Hierarchies are based on bullying and develop where individuals (male or female) have to compete for something they want. If food can be found only in certain areas, for instance, some animals bully others so they have more to eat. And if the only way to move from one place to another is through a gateway, some horses always demand to go first.

Bullying occurs among wild horses but, because they are not confined, victims can keep out of the way of the 'bossy' ones and a dominance hierarchy need not develop.

Among domestic horses harassment can lead to trouble. A horse that hangs back or seems reluctant to go too close to another may be a victim. A young animal introduced into a herd of older horses has to show respect to all the others and it may well be 'bossed' around.

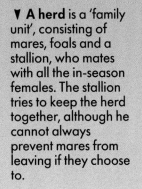

▼ **A herd** is a 'family unit', consisting of mares, foals and a stallion, who mates with all the in-season females. The stallion tries to keep the herd together, although he cannot always prevent mares from leaving if they choose to.

Victims can become unhappy and nervous, bullies over-confident and aggressive. These attitudes affect the way horses react to the humans that look after them.

## Leader of the pack?

Bullies are not necessarily leaders and hierarchies are not associated with leadership. In a herd, although the stallion is the dominant male, a mare may take the lead.

When a herd moves – to find better pasture, for example – one of the mares may decide to leave. Her young follow, and her friends and their young also. The rest of the herd don't want to be left behind so they leave as well.

In response, the stallion tries to herd the mares. He uses special body postures to keep them together if they look as though they are dispersing. He does his best to prevent them from mingling with any other herd they meet in case he loses some of them. But, he is not leader of the herd and does not ultimately decide where they go.

◄ **Close rivals** battle to prove which one is the stronger. The loser, who is 'subordinate', accepts his defeat and submits to the 'dominant' winner.

▼ **When a herd** is on the move, the stallion keeps a close watch on his mares, for fear of losing them to another male.

**Horses** generally live in peace. When the herd has plenty of food and the stallion is not threatened by opposition, there is no need for displays of dominance.

# Stampedes

▲ **If one horse senses danger** the herd bunches together for safety.

Horses have a natural instinct to run from danger. They can out-pace most predators – but only if they notice them soon enough. Any strange smell, movement or sound may mean danger is near.

At the slightest suspicion of such trouble, a horse is alert. He turns to see whether the alarm is real and, unless quickly reassured, it is not long before he flees.

## The running instinct

When grazing or resting peacefully, every member of a herd of wild horses is aware of possible danger, and keeps an eye on his companions. If one horse suddenly stands more erect, with back and neck arched and ears pricked, the other horses may move toward him. That horse has sensed something unwelcome and the herd bunches together for safety.

If one horse starts to run they all run. The herd is in a panic because indi-

viduals may not be able to see clearly where they are going. A stampeding herd tramples down or crashes through any obstacle it meets that is not large and solid enough to stop it. They keep close together, sometimes touching or bumping, and running blindly until the panic is over. By that time they may have travelled a long way. Then they spread out, slow down, and eventually stop.

Domesticated horses have never lost this running instinct. A stampede can sometimes start almost by itself, as horses gallop about when they are playing. Suddenly their happy excitement turns to panic, and the game becomes a stampede. Such 'false' stampedes rarely last more than a few minutes but there is always a risk that individuals could be injured in the rush.

## From gallop to stampede

Unless they are kept well under control by their riders, horses galloping together can all too easily start a stampede. When a single horse panics, he bolts. A herd of bolting horses makes a stampede and is much more serious because the panic of each individual affects the others.

Cavalry charges, with a large number of mounted soldiers advancing on the enemy at full gallop, often turned into an uncontrollable mass of terrified horses.

Horses that are well cared for and know they are safe in familiar surroundings are unlikely ever to stampede, but they must feel they could run for their lives if danger threatened.

Horses need space, for their sense of security as much as for exercise. Allow a horse out whenever possible so he can meet and play with others in the open.

▲ **Domesticated horses** feel secure once they know that humans are their friends and ordinary dogs are not wolves.

▼ **Running in play** is instinctive to horses, but happy galloping can all too quickly turn into panic stampeding.

# What the horse does all day

Left to their own devices, horses are the laziest animals. Their favourite activity is doing nothing at all! But life in the wild is never so easy.

## Eating habits

Wild horses eat a wide variety of vegetation, but because none of it is very nutritious, they have to eat a great deal. They feed in bouts, usually lasting a few hours, then rest to digest the meal before starting to feed again.

The length and frequency of their feeding bouts depend on the quality of the food, and this in turn is affected by the time of year. But horses have no fixed daily routine – they eat when they want to, whether it is day or night.

## Sleep easy

Sleeping, like feeding, takes place in bouts. Despite their love of idleness, horses sleep for only five or so hours in every 24, and only about 30 minutes of this is spent lying down. A horse on the ground is at a disadvantage if danger threatens – it takes longer for him to react and run to safety.

## Togetherness

When they are not feeding or sleeping, wild horses spend much of their time socializing. Grooming is a favourite activity among friends, and takes place several times a day for a few minutes each time. In summer, you can often see them standing head to tail, whisking flies from each other's faces.

Although horses keep to no strict timetable, they tend to take part in the same activities at the same time each day. And whatever they do, they all do together – with one or two of them keeping a lookout for danger. If they feel like a change,

▼**Horses** spend a good part of their day socializing with each other. They love to be among friends and feel safety in numbers.

◄By nature, horses are happiest when they are doing very little. Resting is a favourite activity, especially between feeding bouts.

Overleaf: Horses spend much of their time eating. They feed whenever they are hungry, during the day or night.

however, horses will often introduce variations into their routine.

## Entertainment

In the wild, adult horses rarely play, but for colts and fillies it is one of the main occupations of the day. Their games consist mainly of exploring and running away from imaginary dangers.

In-season mares provide interest not only for the adult stallions but also for the young males. The other mares take little notice, and the mothers are busy watching over their own foals.

## The domesticated horse

It is easy to impose a routine on a domesticated horse by feeding and exercising him at regular times. The best timetable reflects natural behaviour, with events spaced evenly through the day and night. Given the choice, though, every domesticated horse would live in the same way as his wild relations.

▼Youngsters spend a lot of time playing. But play-fighting and running from make-believe dangers are more than just games — they are a rehearsal for adult life.

# And so to bed

In the wild, horses and ponies are part of nature's food chain and are hunted by day and night. A herd must be on constant look-out for predators and time spent sleeping is time spent at risk.

## Caught napping

Horses sleep for about four to five hours out of 24 and in short periods, from ten to 30 minutes long. More than this would increase the possible danger to them from predators.

Short bursts of sleep are also safer for any animals with the same general design as a horse: if it lay on its side for longer than about half an hour, the horse's considerable weight would 'squash' the lung on the ground side. Even when there is no immediate threat, a sleeping horse must stir and shift its weight from one side to another.

Domestic horses have exactly the same sleep patterns and habits as wild horses. In fact, they probably have a more peaceful existence and get more uninterrupted periods of sleep. However they do have one disadvantage: they must adapt to what their owners want. Your horse may just have settled down for an afternoon nap when you decide you want to go for a ride.

All horses, wild and domesticated,

▼ **Domesticated horses** still retain the instinct for self-protection and, like their wild cousins, take it in turns to sleep. One or two horses always remain standing 'on guard' against predators.

take it in turns to sleep. Depending on the size of the herd, there are usually one or two standing up on watch, while the others rest. Even in a line of looseboxes, one or two horses remain standing. When one gets up, another automatically lies down.

## How the horse sleeps

Horses are able to sleep, or doze, in three different positions: standing up; lying down, 'propped' on their breast bone; and flat on their sides. Getting up from either of the lying down positions is quite a performance, involving several vital seconds. But horses dozing on their

feet can quickly spring into action and flee from danger.

There is a special locking arrangement of ligaments in a horse's elbow and stifle joints which prevents him from falling over while dozing. The elbows always lock and the front legs act as stiff props. Often, only one stifle (equivalent to our knee) locks, and the other back leg rests, with the hip down.

## Deep sleep or dozing?

There are two kinds of sleep, SWS (shortwave sleep) and REM sleep (rapid eye movement sleep). During SWS the horse is only lightly asleep. He takes this sort of sleep standing or propped on his breast bone. Sometimes his head drops almost to his knees when he is dozing on his feet. If he is lying down, his muzzle may rest on the ground.

The other kind of sleep is believed to be when horses dream – causing their rapid eye movements. The brain is very active, and the body often twitches as if the horse were dreaming. This is very deep sleep from which it is hard to arouse a pony.

REM sleep is essential to a horse's well-being and can only be taken lying flat out. You must ensure that a horse's stable is large enough for him to lie down flat and get up without banging into walls. A horse that dare not lie on his side becomes tired and irritable – just as we do when we lack sleep! Only if he gets the proper amount of sleep, can a horse remain contented and in good health.

▲ In contrast to horses, orang-utans have no natural enemies. They can relax and sleep soundly for hours on end without fear of being hunted.

They stretch out high in jungle trees, in nests made of leaves and vines.

**DID YOU KNOW?**
When horses are flat out, fast asleep, they sometimes snore, just like humans!

Once they are on their feet after a deep sleep, they often have a good stretch to flex their muscles. They reach both hindlegs out behind them, one at a time, and arch their backs and necks.

# Living through the seasons

In the wild, ponies may have to adapt to extreme weather conditions: long, freezing winters, when plants are covered in snow and ice, and hot, dry summers when droughts may occur.

### The start of winter

As winter approaches, cold-blooded horses and most ponies grow thicker coats. The longer hairs trap an insulating layer of air close to their skin.

Cold, even freezing weather, causes all but the most refined breeds little discomfort, provided they can shelter from the wind and keep dry.

If the pony's coat becomes wet, however, the hairs cling together and the layer of warmed air is lost. Caked mud has the same effect: the coat can no longer provide insulation.

When the wind blows, heat may be carried away from the skin very fast indeed. This is called the 'chill factor'. Horses don't mind frost and snow but they do need shelter against both the rain and the wind.

In the wild, horses find a suitable place to spend the winter and only move from it if they have to. This is because exercise uses up warmth-giving energy which they gain from their food. If food is scarce horses must save their energy for emergencies. They *don't* need to exercise for warmth.

**Caked mud** matts the coat together. This prevents air being trapped between the hairs to keep the pony warm.

### Autumn changes

In autumn grass wilts, forming a brown mat. It looks like hay and horses may eat it if no evergreen leaves are available, though it has little food value.

Horses need large amounts of this poor fare to supply them with enough energy. What they eat is then supplemented by the body breaking down fat stored earlier in the year.

▼ **In summer** ponies take exercise and graze in the coolest parts of the day. In the evening and early morning they are less likely to be bothered by insects.

▲ **Springtime** heralds the growth of lush grass and ponies need to rebuild the food reserves they have used up during winter. *Over*-eating fresh, green grass, on the other hand, can cause the pony just as many problems as undernourishment.

## Spring is in the air

Spring sees renewed plant growth and a new problem. The young grass is richly nutritious and the horses are hungry. If they eat too much too quickly they can suffer badly from colic. However, they must eat to replace the body weight lost during the winter.

In summer, horses find it difficult to keep cool because they have such large bodies. They need shade in the middle of the day and feed mainly when it is coolest – early morning, evening and during the night.

While resting, horses may be badly troubled by biting insects. The tail is an effective fly switch and two friends often stand nose to tail to protect each others' faces from irritation.

In summer horses travel from one pasture to another, but unless frightened or excited they move slowly, saving energy and keeping cool.

▼ **In winter** horses seek shelter from the elements. They only move around if it's absolutely necessary, because they must save their energy.

PART FOUR
—
# HEALTH
# AND FITNESS

# Health and fitness

▲ **When horses** are feeling well they like to socialize with their friends.

Unlike a human being, a pony cannot tell us when he feels ill, so we have to rely on signs, such as his appearance and behaviour, to find out whether he is fit and healthy.

## Healthy signs

If a pony feels healthy he looks healthy. His eyes are bright and he has a glossy coat, he is alert and interested in his surroundings and he socializes with other ponies. He eats and drinks freely and his droppings are normal, depending on how he is kept (green and quite loose if he is at grass, light brown and crumbly if he is hay fed).

When a pony is in good health all his systems work well: his food is thoroughly digested so that his body is nourished, and any waste products are eliminated properly and regularly.

## Signs of poor health

An unhealthy pony often looks dejected, with a dull coat and eyes. He has no

★ **COAT SIGNS**
A good indicator of a pony's health is the state of his coat. It grows from the fatty layer beneath his skin, which is nourished and maintained by the bloodstream. If his coat is dull it is a tell-tale sign that the pony's body systems are not working properly.

❗ **STABLE CONDITION**
A vital factor in a horse's health and fitness is fresh air. The stable must be well ventilated as horses have sensitive respiratory systems. Always leave the top door of your pony's stable open and turn him out into a field as often as possible.

▼ **This Arab's coat** has a healthy shine to it – a sure sign he is in good condition.

energy and shows no interest in his surroundings or in playing with other ponies. A sick pony usually has little appetite and thirst.

His pulse, respiration rate and temperature are often abnormal (his pulse rate is normally 36-42 beats per minute, his respiration rate 8-14 times a minute and his temperature is about 38°C/100.4°F.)

These symptoms are signs that disease is interfering with the normal body functions. When disease affects a pony his body uses much of his energy to fight off the illness. This leaves little strength for keeping all of his body systems in full working order.

## Fighting fit

When a pony is fit he is well 'muscled up' – he has firmer muscles and looks trimmer than an unfit one. He is alert and does not tire easily, provided he's ridden sensibly. After a workout his pulse and respiration rates return to their normal

speeds within about 10 minutes of him stopping and resting.

Fitness is achieved by a careful combination of gradually increased exercise and feeding. The additional food provides the extra energy a pony needs to cope with the strenuous work you give him. As he works harder and eats more he becomes fitter and all his body systems function correctly.

▲ **Healthy horses** eat at their leisure. Their food is properly digested and the waste products passed out.

▼ **By careful feeding and exercising** a horse reaches peak fitness.

# Speed and athletic ability

Athletic performance in the wild is usually dependent on fear: a horse speeds away or jumps obstacles when he feels threatened. He inherits his athletic ability from his ancestors, who developed physically according to the terrain of the land they lived in.

## Running wild

Horses gallop to escape from their enemies, but the safest horse is not necessarily the one that runs fastest. Safety in numbers is the hard and fast rule for survival in the wild.

When wild horses flee from danger, they are not trying to see who can run fastest. The entire herd runs together. What matters most of all is the ability to keep up with the herd. The horse that lags behind is vulnerable, but so, too, is the one that outstrips the rest. Eventually, he tires and may find himself alone and defenceless.

## Natural athletes

Man makes use of the horse's natural athletic qualities by training domesticated animals to jump fences and race against one another.

Some breeds are better racers or jumpers than others (although there are always exceptional individuals). These differences are inherited from the original wild horses, who developed different characteristics according to the surroundings they inhabited.

In some places, forests bordered on the grasslands where the horses grazed. When these horses ran for safety, they headed for the shelter of the trees where they could hide. They had to be able to run fast, but not far.

Other habitats were wide open plains with no shelter nearby. Horses living on these plains had to rely on their speed and stamina to outrun predators.

## Best of both worlds

In some regions, the homelands of herds of different types of horse overlapped. Shelter-seekers and long-distance runners met and interbred. This meant that their offspring inherited characteristics from both herds.

Horses with a mixture of different ancestors are more likely to produce widely differing foals. This is because the characteristics of one generation may not appear in their offspring, but will resurface in a later generation.

A horse may surprise everyone by displaying talents its breed is not supposed to possess. The offspring of a draught horse sometimes turns out to be an excel-

▼ **Wild horses** must stay as a group when they run from danger. Those members that outstrip or lag behind the herd are the most vulnerable to predators.

lent jumper because of a warm-blooded ancestor. In just the same way, human children sometimes inherit the hair colouring of a grandparent or great-grandparent rather than that of one of their own parents.

## All shapes and sizes

Speed and agility depend for a large part on physical characteristics. A horse with long legs and a supple back can usually outrun one with short legs and a stiff back. A jumper has to have strong hindquarters to propel him upward. But a horse's physical appearance is not always such a reliable indication of his athletic ability.

It may be true that heavily built horses are unlikely to win races against Thoroughbreds, but horses of many types and breeds, shapes and sizes can compete against each other in show-jumping events with equal chances of success.

A horse's athletic ability is also dictated by his temperament. For a horse to compete well in public he must be able to keep calm and ignore distracting noises, bright lights and excitement. A show jumper needs courage and confidence in his rider. A racehorse must remain unaffected by the crowds or the other horses around him.

▲ The Thoroughbred's tremendous speed and athleticism are determined by ancestry and breeding. Few horses match their performance on the flat.

◄ Although a show jumper has to be strong and athletic, no one breed reigns supreme — successful jumpers come in all shapes and sizes.

# Speed and stamina

The horse deals with danger by running away from it. Its reaction to a threat, or anything it thinks might be a threat, is to move out of range. That is why a horse can be so difficult to catch!

## Hunting and hunted

Animals that hunt for their food and those they hunt (like the horse) often evolve together. The hunt is frequently based on chasing. When the prey manages to run a little faster, the hunter must also increase its speed, which means the prey must run more rapidly still.

How long the prey can run for matters as much as speed, however, and the horse is not the fastest of all animals. It makes up for this by having great stamina. Provided it can start running before the enemy is too close, it can stay out of reach until the enemy is exhausted and has to stop.

At their fastest pace, the gallop, most horses run at about 50kmph (30mph). Unlike its natural enemies, the horse can maintain a gallop – the equivalent of a sprint – for several miles.

## Built for speed

The maximum speed any runner can reach depends partly on the length of stride, which is why the fastest human athletes usually have long legs. The horse also has very long legs.

Because they must carry the weight of the animal the lower *bones* of its legs are longer than the upper bones. The large *muscles* are concentrated in the upper leg, close to the shoulders and pelvis, as

▼ **The fastest racehorses** can run at about 65kmph (40mph).

But, despite careful breeding and racetrack improvements, horses today don't run much faster than they did 50 years ago!

they do the hard work. The feet are as small as it has been possible for evolution to make them.

All of this saves energy, because the parts of the body that move furthest as the legs swing back and forth – the lower legs and feet – weigh very little.

The harder an animal works, the more oxygen and the bigger the blood supply its muscles need. The horse has a large chest and lungs, so it can take in plenty of air at each breath, and a powerful heart. This pumps the blood around the body, and the rate of the heart beat increases from about 35 times a minute at rest to over 200 for galloping.

The combination of leg, chest and muscle power makes the horse a formidable runner.

## Chest note

The horse's chest should be wide enough to allow for a good lung capacity and plenty of heart space. This is essential for a fast runner over long distances.

A narrow chest shows poor conformation and suggests that the horse lacks quality and power.

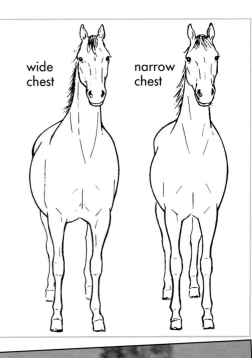

wide chest    narrow chest

▲ **Hot-bloods,** such as the Arab, can run fast because they have long, fine legs and well-proportioned bodies.

▼ **Cold-bloods** are slower than lighter breeds because they have heavy bodies and their legs are relatively short.

# Body-weight and temperature

▼ Even in freezing cold weather a healthy horse's body temperature remains normal.

The horse's body-weight and temperature are good indications of his overall condition. Keeping a close eye on both is the key to owning a healthy pony.

## Body heat

Although horses are divided into hot-bloods, warm-bloods and cold-bloods, the body temperature of all healthy horses is around 37.5-38.3°C (99-101°F). It rarely extends beyond this range.

During a cold night, when a horse is inactive, his temperature may fall by half a degree. If his body temperature drops several degrees below normal the horse is seriously ill.

A slight rise in temperature may follow a period of strenuous exercise, but more often it indicates an infectious type of illness. If your pony's temperature rises more than half a degree for no obvious reason, call in the vet.

## Body-weight

It is sometimes difficult to be sure at a glance how much your pony weighs. One of the best guides is to look at his ribs – they should not stand out but should be easily felt through the skin.

Horses aren't all meant to look exactly the same, though. Like humans, some ponies are naturally fatter than others. Keeping your pony healthy is a question of maintaining his body-weight at the level that suits his lifestyle and his build.

## Too fat or too thin

A pony's weight is determined by the amount of food he eats and how much he exercises – active horses tend to carry less body fat than inactive animals. Extremes, or sudden changes, of body-weight can be a sign of ill health.

If a pony is excessively overweight any work he does puts a strain on his whole body, especially his heart and legs. Horses that are too thin do not have ade-

quate fat reserves to convert into energy for activity or to keep themselves warm in winter.

Ponies are most likely to be overweight if they are given too much food for the amount of work they do.

There can be several reasons why a pony is underweight. He could be a 'poor doer' (his body is inefficient at converting food into fat stores). He may be underfed or have digestive or dental problems.

If a pony has worms in his intestines, they remove the nutrients from his food before his body has a chance to absorb them. Diarrhoea also prevents proper nutrient absorption. Diseases of the liver or kidneys allow too many nutrients to be passed out so the pony becomes malnourished and loses weight.

## *On a diet*

If you are advised to alter your pony's diet, avoid making rapid changes, or colic could be the result.

If you are cutting down a stabled pony's feed intake, give small quantities of meadow hay and molassed chaff, or keep him inside (not on straw) during the day and turn him out to graze at night – this way he is likely to eat less. Steady exercise – about two hours of walking or trotting each day – helps weight loss and keeps a pony trim.

Don't reduce the amount of feed

drastically. If you starve your pony, you can do him serious damage. When a pony's rations are cut suddenly his body breaks down fat reserves to provide him with energy. Increased levels of fat particles in the blood can lead to liver and kidney damage.

Rapid increases in feed intake are also dangerous. Increasing your pony's bodyweight by giving him access to too much lush pasture puts him in grave danger of developing laminitis.

◄ **If you are trying to alter** your pony's weight you should take expert advice about his diet. Any changes in feeding should be made gradually to avoid colic.

**DID YOU KNOW?**
Foals and small ponies have higher temperatures than adults and bigger horses. When a foal is born his temperature is around 38.9°C (102°F). It begins to drop two or three days after he is born, and by the time he is three years old it is steady between 37.5-38.3°C (99-101°F).

★ **HEATING FOODS**
Body temperature is not affected by 'over-heating' foods, such as oats. They simply provide more energy and make the horse more active.

◄ **A sure sign** that a pony is in good condition is the covering of flesh over his ribs. You should be able to feel his ribs easily under the skin but they should not stick out.

# Shock and trauma

Shock and trauma in a horse's life are closely linked. Trauma is when something upsetting or frightening happens to him. And when a horse suffers from trauma, he can go into a state of shock.

## Surprise attack

Trauma can be anything that scares a horse. It can be an event that happens without warning, a road accident, for example, or it may be something planned, such as an operation.

## Scared of school

Individual horses are frightened by different situations. However, there are some things which will traumatize (upset or frighten) most horses. These are falls on slippery roads or accidents over jumps, collisions with cars, attacks by dogs or bully horses in the field, stressful schooling sessions, or overwork. Illnesses and operations can be traumatic even when the horse is under anaesthetic and doesn't know what is going on. He may still be traumatized when he wakes up after surgery.

## Shocking state

A traumatized horse goes quickly into a state of shock. The cause of the trauma may be mental, but the effects are very physical. When a horse is in shock, his blood pressure drops, his heart beats faster and weaker, and his blood tends to circulate in the centre of his body, leaving the extremities, such as his head and legs, short of blood.

## Cold sweat

He either breathes very slowly or pants rapidly like a dog. He may feel unwell and come out in patchy, cold sweats. His mucous membranes (the moist lining inside the nose, eyes and mouth) become pale, greyish or bluish instead of their normal healthy salmon pink. It is important to recognize these danger signs because shock can be treated successfully if you call the vet in time.

If your horse goes into shock, put him in a well bedded-down stable with good ventilation as soon as possible. Rug him up and keep him extra warm by putting woollen stable bandages on his legs.

▼ **Battles between stallions** in the wild can be a frightening enough spectacle for humans, let alone for the horses themselves. One or both of the combatants may suffer severe trauma from the attack and go into shock for a long time. It is possible for a horse to die from really deep shock, especially in the wild where there is no vet to treat him.

NEWTON LE WILLOWS
LIBRARY
TEL. 01744 677885/86/?

Be calm and keep him quiet. Try to keep noisy people and dogs well away from him and turn off radios in the vicinity of the stable.

## Vet's solution

When the vet arrives, she may give your horse an injection to stimulate his circulation and to calm him down. Other fluids may be injected intravenously (into a vein), such as blood plasma, saline solution, or antibiotics. He may also be given oxygen through a mask.

Ask the vet for strict instructions about feeding. You will probably be advised to give your horse small, easily digested feeds when he calms down after his initial recovery.

## Shock treatment

Ask the vet about watering, stable management and exercise. You must follow these instructions as a horse can go back into shock if not treated properly.

Shock and trauma can be serious, so you should learn the symptoms and call the vet if you suspect shock.

▲ **An unsuccessful jump** causes trauma for most horses. Even when he is not hurt physically after an accident, a horse may go into shock if he has an upsetting experience such as this.

**Overleaf:** It may take a long time for a horse to recover from a shocking experience. Once he has got over the initial trauma, it may be a good idea to keep him in the company of another calm horse such as this British Riding Pony, to help rebuild his confidence.

◄ **The vet** may administer an injection to a horse in shock to get his blood circulation going and to calm him down gradually.

# Coping with boredom

In the wild, horses are fully occupied eating, socializing with other herds or moving from one grazing ground to another. They don't have time to be bored. For domesticated animals, it can be a different matter.

## Domestic bliss?

There is often not enough to keep a domestic pony mentally and physically occupied. When he is stabled he can suffer from too little exercise and not enough hay to feed on over a long period. Stabled ponies sometimes have to spend many hours a day with nothing to do.

Even field-kept ponies may not have enough space to take truly natural exercise and enjoy a change of view. If they share a field there may not be much to eat and boredom can result.

▼ **Company** is most important for horses: they are social animals and need to be among friends.

Bored horses *look* fed-up. Their eyes are not focused on anything in particular, their ears are at 'half mast', flopping toward the sides and slightly back, and their nostrils are drawn back a little.

They often stand moping, close to the nearest source of entertainment, such as a gate or a road. If they are in a stable they may stand at the back of the box or with their tails to the door.

Constant boredom can cause depression and a soured temperament. This is particularly noticeable in racehorses and hard-worked competition horses, both of which are often stabled for long periods. But single ponies at grass can also become unhappy and depressed, through lack of company.

Sensitive, highly bred animals, with a good deal of Arab or Thoroughbred ▶

►**To keep a stabled pony occupied** make sure he has a full hay net at all times. A toy, such as a football in a net, gives him something to play with and stops boredom setting in.

▼ **Wild horses** rarely have time to become bored. Usually, they are too busy looking for new grazing grounds or eating.

blood, are the most likely to become easily bored. They like to know what's going on and prefer to be near the centre of activity and their friends.

## Preventing boredom

Boredom and frustration are thought to cause stable vices and many experts believe that some horses (though not so often ponies) copy vices from one another. However, it's more likely that if conditions in a yard cause *one* animal to develop a vice they'll affect *the others* badly, too.

Boredom can be prevented by giving a pony plenty to amuse him. Naturally, he should eat most of the time, so make sure he has enough grazing. When he's

stabled, ensure he has a constant supply of hay.

Give him a really full net if you're going to leave him for many hours and use one that has small holes, so it takes him longer to eat.

Ideally, keep the pony on a combined system rather than fully stabled, and give him plenty of ridden or driven work on varied routes to spark his interest.

Company is especially important as ponies need to mix with others. Grilled 'chat holes' between individual stables stop them feeling so isolated.

One of the golden rules of horse management is to let your pony have plenty to occupy him, whether he is stabled or out.

▼ **Domestic animals** need plenty of exercise. Vary your hacking route every so often, to make sure your pony has a change of scenery and stays alert.

# Stable manners

▲ **If your pony** is happy and comfortable in his box, and is used to a daily routine, good stable manners should be easy for him to learn.

Horses and ponies do not automatically know what is correct behaviour – good stable manners – and what is not. Like dogs, they have to be trained, and the best time to do this is when they are young.

## What the pony has to know

The pony must become used to being handled all over – for grooming, tacking up and veterinary treatment. He must lift, and keep up, his feet for picking out and shoeing, and move over when asked. He should stand still for mounting and dismounting, and move forward or back as required. He should also learn to come to you when you call his name – most ponies are not taught this.

He must also learn what *not* to do, such as biting, kicking and milling around when you want him to keep still.

## The right frame of mind

It takes time to make a pony understand what you want. It takes even more time, and patience, to bring him to the state of mind where he does the right thing almost as a reflex action.

A pony needs to be calm to learn. An excited or frightened pony thinks only of self preservation.

You must be firm and confident, but at the same time gentle and quiet. The pony then trusts and respects you and is able to pick up commands more quickly than if you bark them out aggressively.

You also have to be consistent, always behaving in the same way. Make requests with the same vocal commands or touches on his body each time. As far as possible, always do your stable chores in the same order, sticking to a routine. That way your pony knows what to expect and feels safe because he is aware of what's coming next.

## Timing

Stable manners are best learned during foalhood, before the foal grows too wild and strong for you to control.

◄**When you are leading** your pony in-hand, he should walk forward willingly but calmly, without barging. Don't allow him to hang back so you have to pull him; this is an equally bad habit.

If your pony is grown up and has learnt bad ways, it is possible to teach him better stable manners. Don't feel defeated, however, if the training is more difficult, takes up more time, and calls for expert help.

There are many cases of badly behaved animals changing owners and becoming reformed characters in new hands. Unfortunately, the reverse is also true! Once you have taught your pony, keep up the good work and insist that he maintains your standards.

## How to train him

Remember, the pony doesn't speak English: you have to *show* him what you want by various touches, pushes and pulls on his body. At the same time you have to use the vocal command for what you want, so he comes to associate that sound – the word itself means nothing to him – with that particular movement. Always say the command in exactly the same way. Your pony should learn to co-operate while the following tasks are being performed.

**Picking up feet:** It's easier to start with a hindfoot as the pony only carries a third of his weight on his back half. He can still see you, although you're 'at the back'.

Run your hand from his withers, along his back and quarters and down his hindleg in the usual way. When you reach the fetlock, grasp his feather (if he has any) or hold the fetlock firmly with both hands. At the same time, push his thigh fairly hard with your shoulder and

weight, pull the fetlock up and slightly back and say 'up'.

*Say nothing else*, even if you don't succeed. Repeat the process exactly. When you achieve just a little lift, praise him at once even if he puts the foot straight down again. Leave it at that for the first lesson. With practice over a few days, he'll soon catch on.

**Shoeing:** Before the farrier comes for the first time, the pony must be used to you lifting and picking out his feet. Practise

★ **OLDER PONIES**
If you have an older pony who is bad mannered, teach him good behaviour in exactly the same way as a young one. It takes a long time, but if you are consistent and keep to a routine he can learn, you'll succeed in the end. If you feel he is too much for you, consult your instructor before giving up.

Remember that thrashings won't work. Sympathetic, firm correction does, but it must be done *immediately* for the pony to associate it with whatever he did wrong.

◄ **Your pony must be taught** early in his training to stand quietly when tethered. Remember always to tie the lead-rope in an easy-release slip knot, so that you can free him if he should panic.

► **When lifting a foreleg,** run your hand firmly down from the elbow before grasping the feather on the fetlock. It's an extra help if you also push behind his knee with your elbow. This encourages him to bend the joint and lift the foot.

▼ **Once you have trained** your pony to lift his feet without fuss, he is ready for his first meeting with the farrier. The pony must also be able to keep a foot up while it is being trimmed or shod. A pony that fidgets excessively during shoeing is a danger to himself and the farrier.

tapping the ground surface of the hoof wall with the hoof pick handle (to imitate nailing on).

**Grooming:** Look on this as an extension of stroking. Always speak in a reassuring voice and praise him for being good when you groom him. Don't insist too much at first if he objects to, say, his head being done.

**Clipping:** The noise of the clippers often upsets ponies. For some days before you want to use them, run the clippers in the yard, getting gradually nearer the pony's box. When he seems calm, take the clippers into the box, but have an expert with you. Talk soothingly and stroke your pony. Rest the clipper head on your hand as you stroke him, then gently place the clippers directly on his body.

It's best to let your expert clip the difficult areas although there's no point insisting if the pony plays up greatly. Racehorses' heads are quite often left unclipped because it upsets them too much.

**Standing still:** Fidgety ponies are a real nuisance. They must learn to stand still for grooming and handling, mounting and dismounting.

Start the training in the stable before moving out into the open, and have a friend with you if possible. Stand the pony in the middle of the box and say 'stand' – nothing else. The instant he moves out of position say 'no!' in a firm voice without shouting, and put him back where he was. Say 'stand' again. As long as he does, say 'good boy' and give him a titbit. When he moves, again say 'no', replace him, say 'stand' and praise him.

He should learn from the tone of your voice that standing still is good and moving around is not. He'll pick up and learn the sounds, and associate 'good boy' with titbits.

**Moving over:** This is most important. Standing still is fine but you don't want him rooted in one place when you're trying to work around him!

The command to use is 'over'. Have a friend or expert with you at first. If you want the pony to move to the right, stand on his left. Place the flat of your hands on his side (where your leg would go when riding), with one hand above the other just behind the girth area. Stiffen your arms slightly and swing your weight on to them, pushing on his side. At the same time, say 'over'.

Repeat this a few times, but don't be impatient, he'll get the message eventually. The moment he takes even one step over, say 'good boy' in an approving tone. Eventually, you'll be able to touch him lightly, say 'over', and he'll step quickly to one side.

Placing your hands where your leg goes reinforces your riding aids. When the pony feels pressure just behind the girth, from either leg or hand, he knows he has to step away from the pressure, not fight it.

## Know your pony

You have to strike a balance between creating a well-mannered, happy pony and a 'machine' who daren't step out of line. Your pony learns to be obedient only if you make his lessons enjoyable. Good behaviour, learned through confident, firm but sympathetic handling, is essential. A strong animal like a pony cannot be allowed to do as he pleases. On the other hand, ponies must be allowed to express their characters if they are to feel contented – just like humans.

With time, the pony comes to know how far he can go, and behaves and helps you when it really matters. You reach this relationship only by spending time with him, communicating with him and showing him that you won't be taken advantage of, but that you care enough to teach him good manners.

▲ **It's very important** to teach a young pony from the start to stand still while you are grooming him. Remember always to be gentle when brushing; roughness can turn what should be an enjoyable experience into an ordeal.

◄ **Ill-fitting tack** is a common reason for a pony's misbehaviour when being saddled. If you're worried about your pony's tack fitting comfortably, ask an expert to check it over for you.

# Problems round the yard

Most ponies have some aspect of their behaviour which is not as their owners would wish – some 'quirk' such as disliking red buses, refusing to go through water or playing up at the sight of an umbrella. Because we can't ask ponies outright what's bothering them, we have to work out for ourselves what to do about these problems and vices.

## A mental block

Although some problems are caused by naughtiness, most are the result of fear, or at least apprehension. Probably some thing or person in the past has hurt or frightened the pony and he now associates a particular place or process with pain, fear or discomfort. He acts up in anticipation of more of the same, or in self-defence.

If the pony is badly worried, he may appear to develop a mental block. He doesn't pay normal attention to his rider's aids or voice and may seem rooted to the spot in apparent fear, perhaps trembling. Scientists call this extreme fear 'tonic immobility'.

Most problems, though, are not that bad, and if you try to understand *why* the pony is behaving as he is you are half way to a cure.

## Difficult with saddlery

Ponies that don't like being tacked up may associate saddlery with work, but it is usually because someone has been rough. Re-training the pony by doing everything carefully, not in a rush, and talking calmly to him, helps greatly.

▼ **Vices** are more often brought about by human mis-handling than by a horse's bad character. Correct stable management in a well-ordered environment is a major step toward avoiding potential problems.

With headshy ponies, try standing on a strong crate so you can reach over the ears. Before you start, unbuckle the reins at the 'rider' end. Pass one rein up each shoulder from under his neck and buckle them again. Bring the buckle up to his poll, giving yourself control of his head. Putting the bridle together on his head sometimes works.

When unbridling, undo the curb chain (if worn), noseband and throat-lash. Hold one end of the bit to steady it and let him drop the mouthpiece in his own time. If necessary, persuade him to open his mouth by tickling his tongue through the corner of his mouth with your thumb or finger. *Never* snatch the bit out as this painful process may well have been the cause of the problem in the first place.

If the saddle is the problem, tie up the pony beforehand. Talk to him and *don't* girth up quickly or all at once, which is a major cause of trouble. Always be gentle and, if the pony becomes nasty or violent, ask an experienced person to help you.

## Difficult to lead

If the pony hangs back and does not walk smartly in-hand, it is probably due either to laziness or to not having been taught to lead as a foal. Don't try to drag him along like a naughty dog – it doesn't work with ponies. ▶

**▼ Saddle problems:** Before taking the saddle off, loosen the girth a hole or two while you are still mounted, so you don't have to haul at it from the ground to unbuckle it. Remember to make sure that the pony's tack is comfortable and well fitting.

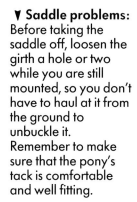

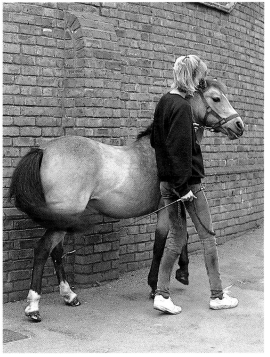

**◀ Practise leading** a difficult pony alongside a wall so he can't move sideways. If he rushes move closer to his head or even just in front of him and say 'whoa' in a deep soothing voice. With a pony who dawdles, give a brisk command 'walk on!' and tap him on the flank.

Gloves should be worn when leading a pony.

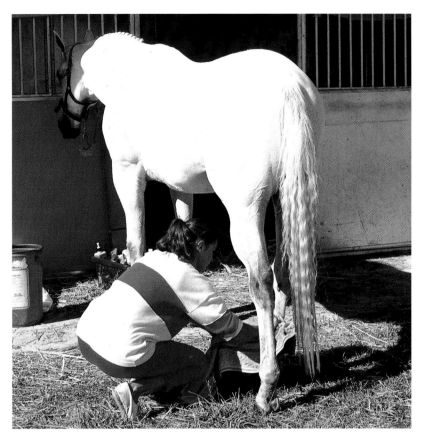

▲ **A pony** who dislikes being groomed may object to stiff, bristly dandy brushes! Persuade him to enjoy grooming by using a towel or stable rubber on sensitive areas.

**❗ FEAR OR FURY**
How you handle a pony who is playing up depends on the cause – stubbornness or genuine fear – and you need to be able to tell the difference.

When a pony is frightened he usually has a wide-eyed look and his nostrils are flared. His neck and other muscles may feel hard and tense and he may snort and tremble. When he is just being stubborn, he does not have a fearful expression. He may look bored or cross. He does not tremble or feel unusually tense either.

Find a wall or strong fence to lead along, and place the pony close up to it. In your free hand carry a schooling whip or strong twig about a metre long.

Stand at the pony's shoulder – *not* in front of him – facing forward, and give the command 'walk on!'. If he doesn't, or he dawdles, give the command again and *at the same time* put your whip hand behind your back and flick him smartly on the flank without looking back. Few ponies fail to jump to it with this startling reinforcement of your vocal request, so be ready!

You may need to give him several lessons – repeating it each time you lead him so he realizes that he must *always* walk out. In a few days you should notice a real improvement. Always give him the chance to obey first, only flicking him if he hangs back.

Rushing and barging, unlike hanging back, are often caused by nerves or by too much food and too little work. If the reason is an awkward nature, reverse the above process to teach the pony manners.

## Bad to groom

Gentleness is the key here. Don't push matters if he is really difficult, and be prepared to use your hands or a cloth instead of a brush.

Rough brushing and being knocked on bony areas such as head or legs, or scrubbed hard in sensitive areas with a stiff dandy brush, are the sort of actions which *cause* trouble.

## Dislike of being tied up

This is quite understandable when you remember that, in the wild, ponies depended on their freedom to escape predators. Domesticated ponies 'recall' this instinct and some panic when they feel restrained.

In some countries, it is felt safest to tie up a horse to a ring via a string loop, which breaks if the pony pulls back in fear. In other countries, it is thought wisest to teach the horse that he *cannot* break free, no matter what.

One thing is sure, once a pony *has* broken free, he knows for the rest of his life that he can do so. Many horses then persistently break loose.

Curing a confirmed case can be practically impossible and is a job for an expert. In other cases, make sure you never leave the tied pony alone, and always use a quick-release knot.

The instant a pony starts to pull back, pat him firmly on the tail and say some command he understands such as 'stand up!' or 'walk on!' to get him forward again and remove the tension from the

▲ **Tie-up:** As the pony pulls back, tap his tail and tell him to walk on. Stand close in case he kicks.

► **If the smoke** and sizzle of hot shoeing cause problems, have the pony cold shod, as racehorses are.

rope. Speak soothingly if he is frightened, maybe of a sudden noise.

If he is simply being awkward, an experienced friend can help you by standing to one side near the tail. As soon as the pony pulls back, the friend reinforces your verbal command by 'scrubbing' him lightly between the buttocks with a stable broom's bristles or a dandy brush. Most ponies – except confirmed cases – stop when they learn to associate pulling back with an uncomfortable scrub!

## Difficult to shoe

This can be a real problem, especially when you have a rough, impatient farrier. If you do, search for another!

As with grooming, kidding the pony along, talking kindly, giving him frequent titbits during the process, and general patience are the cure. Sometimes blinkers can help.

With *any* problem, losing your temper (or allowing someone else to do so), shouting and hitting the pony hard, just make matters worse.

# Stopping stable vices

The term 'stable vices' describes any one of several different ways in which a horse or pony can habitually misbehave in his stable. The habit may harm his health, make him dangerous, or mean he is more difficult to handle. Three of the most common – and troublesome – are weaving, crib-biting and box-walking.

## Why do vices start?

The main cause of almost any vice is some kind of stress, which makes the animal unhappy, edgy or discontented.

It is usually the more finely bred, highly strung animals which suffer – those containing Thoroughbred blood and, less often, Arab blood, being especially prone to 'nerves'. Those with plenty of pony, cob or heavier blood are rarely affected, but there are exceptions.

Generally, any animal with a nervous disposition – one who tends to worry about life – can develop a stable vice.

It is sometimes said that horses copy each other and that vices are catching. However, current research in different countries suggests this is not the case. It is far more likely to be poor stable management which causes the trouble.

## Understanding your pony

Horses and ponies are individuals, like us, and the same living conditions do not

▼ Stabled horses need regular exercise to stop them becoming restless, fidgety, bored and miserable – which is when they're liable to take up a vice.

suit all. Study the pony in your care closely. Find out which conditions make him most contented and ask your vet's advice if you're not sure. A comfortable, peaceful pony is unlikely to be unhappy or need to release inner tension by misbehaving.

For that is what most stable vices are – outlets for anxiety, boredom and misery. Before long, the action becomes a fixed habit and is difficult to stop.

*And punishing a horse for such misbehaviour does not cure the problem.*

## Prevention and cure

Formerly, it was thought best to try to stop the horse performing a vice without asking *why* it was doing so. Now, the approach is to try to manage horses so that they feel happy and do not feel the *need* to behave badly.

Typically, this means regular turning out with companions the horse likes, enough work and exercise, handlers he respects and trusts and a proper feeding regime. The horse should never get very hungry. He is 'designed' to eat most of the time and long periods between meals are unnatural to him.

A constant supply of good hay (except for an hour or two before work) helps here, particularly during the long nights when horses don't sleep right through as humans do.

★ **HABIT FORMING**
Recent research indicates that vices produce natural substances called endorphins which make the horse feel 'high'.

Sadly, endorphins are often habit-forming, and the horse eventually becomes addicted and cannot stop the vice. There are courses of treatment available so discuss these with your vet.

## Box-walking

The affected horse marches endlessly round and round his box, making a track in his bedding or the floor if it is soft enough. A box-walker often seems to be in a daze, like a sleep-walker.

Putting bales of straw in the horse's way or tying him up are often recommended. But these are not the answer as the horse may fall over the bales and injure himself. And, if he is tied up, he will feel more frustrated and miserable than ever. Natural management helps – plenty of exercise and turning out with friends.

## Crib-biting

The horse grips a projection – such as the stable door top – with his teeth. He forms a vacuum in the throat by tensing the muscles, then suddenly releases them, gulping down air with a grunt.

Crib-biting has been said to cause indigestion due to air in the stomach and intestines. In fact, in the early stages the habit is often a *sign* of indigestion. When the diet is improved – usually involving better quality food and/or more hay – the vice often stops.

However, there is no record of a *confirmed* crib-biter or wind-sucker ever having been cured. It is best to prevent any vice starting or try to stop it when first spotted – by checking the diet and introducing more natural management.

▲ **Chewing wood** is often a sign of mineral deficiency which can be put right with a salt lick and food supplements.

► **But when a horse crib-bites,** he doesn't need to *chew*, he just grips with his teeth, arches his neck, draws in breath and gulps while swallowing.

**WIND-SUCKING**
Wind-sucking is a vice similar to crib-biting, but the horse does not need to grip anything. He can form the necessary vacuum on his own.

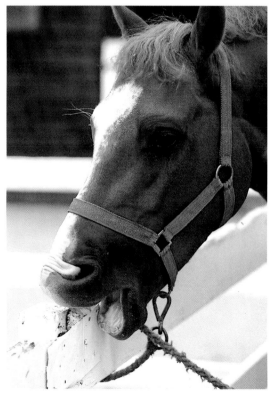

## Cribbing strap

Devices such as cribbing straps (leather straps fitted tightly round the throat, some with a metal projection which 'stabs' the horse when he arches his neck) are not cures. They only prevent the horse from cribbing as long as they are worn.

Similarly, surgery to nick the neck muscles he needs to arch his neck does not get to the root of the problem and stop the horse *wanting* to crib.

### Home-made cures

Two plastic bottles filled with water suspended on either side of the doorway may help deter weaving. They should be one quarter of the way in each side.

▲ **Weaving can be stopped** – but rarely cured, except in the early stages – by fitting a grille to the door.

▼ **Turning horses out to grass** so they enjoy freedom and company is a good way to stop vices.

## Weaving

The horse stands with his head over the stable door and swings his weight from one foreleg to the other, back and forth from side to side. He swings his head in the same direction as the movement.

Zoo animals in cages (particularly elephants) do the same thing. It is thought that claustrophobic horses – who hate being shut in an enclosed space – and those who prefer to be on the move, not stabled, are most prone.

Expert opinion suggests that it is natural for the horse to walk slowly forward moving his head from side to side while he grazes. The horse is 'programmed' to perform this movement in the wild, and weaving is the closest a confined animal can get.

So more sympathetic management and plenty of exercise provide the best and most long-lasting cure.

With most stable vices, there are ways of physically preventing them. But there's more to it than just stopping the horse's action. The aim is to keep your pony contented with his life so he doesn't develop a bad habit in the first place.

## Barging

Barging from and/or into the stable stems from bad manners or fear. With a little expert help, you'll be able to tell whether the horse is frightened (with wide eyes, tense muscles and a general nervousness) or just rude (with a 'don't care' attitude, and a relaxed and confident, 'get-out-of-my-way' manner).

If he's frightened, be confident yourself. Stroke him and talk to him, encourage him to keep his head down and let him take his time. Check him gently if he rushes, with short, repeated tugs on the lead-rope and with firm but not hard slaps on the breast with your hand. Give him a titbit *immediately* he proceeds slowly, so he associates the action with something pleasant.

If he's just rude, give him one sharp

▼ **An interesting view** with plenty of activity going on helps to prevent horses which are bored when stabled from becoming fidgety.

slap across the breast with your whip, a short, firm tug on the lead-rope and a firm command 'whoa!' all at the same time. Keep doing this until he behaves, even if you only go one step at a time at a correct pace. You may need a strong adult to restrain him initially, and a bridle to give more control than a headcollar. Don't give titbits if he's bad tempered.

## Banging and kicking

Some horses knock repeatedly against the stable door with their front feet, making loud banging noises. The habit not only annoys other horses and humans, but it seriously damages stables. It can also lame the horse by jarring his feet and legs and bruising his joints, which results in swelling and soreness.

Kicking the wall with the hindfeet is usually in response to the frustration of being locked up and given too little freedom and exercise, combined with too much food.

Horses generally bang and kick because they want something such as attention, freedom, food, companionship or exercise. Young horses often do both until they become used – or resigned – to being stabled, even if just stabled at night. Many older horses only bang after a long period of confinement such as first thing in the morning or on a boring day off.

In both cases, try to remove the cause. Give the horse plenty to do and turn him out as much as possible. Take note of when and apparently why he bangs or kicks and try to prevent those circumstances. For a horse who bangs at feed time, for instance, give him his meal first if there are other ponies also being fed. If he bangs when a friend is going out, distract him for a while, and so on.

## Climbing over the door

This vice can be stopped by fitting a bar or grille in the top half of the stable door, and that may be your only remedy. But ask yourself *why* and *when* he does it and try to avoid those circumstances.

Some horses climb because they can't tolerate being stabled, in which case, do consider management systems involving the minimum of stabling, if any. If, on the other hand, the situations which cause climbing are momentary, such as

▼ **Frustrated with his confinement** to a stable, a horse is quite likely to pass the time with a habit such as wood chewing and this can quickly develop into a confirmed vice.

▼ **Stable management:** Companionship, fresh air, a comfortable bed, and plenty of good-quality food and water are essential to keep horses contented with life.

▼ Some horses only bang, kick or climb over the stable door to gain attention at certain times – when a friend is led out for exercise, for instance. In such cases, try to distract the horse for a while by giving him his feed or grooming him.

A grille (inset) stops the horse climbing over the door but does not remove his desire to do so.

a friend passing by, shut the top door for a few minutes only.

A few horses actually jump out of their stables, and can fracture their withers or injure their legs or heads; others manage to half jump and half clamber over the door. It's obviously dangerous (particularly if you're just outside the door when it happens), and should be prevented if at all possible.

## Nipping over the door

The horse puts his ears back suddenly and lunges as you pass the stable or when you try to open his door. Some stop short and only threaten, but others

make contact, which is very painful!

Nipping is due to bad temper, nervousness or impatience. Stallions do this naturally to establish dominance. A bar or grille means the horse can't get at you but doesn't make him feel any happier. As always, more sympathetic management greatly reduces the habit – remove the cause and let him out and about more.

In the short term, say 'no' in a cross tone (but don't shout) when the horse nips. Alternatively, throwing a bucket of water over him when he lunges sometimes does the trick.

Smacking his muzzle *may* work if you

do it at once, but may also make him headshy and he could bang his head on the door lintel as he draws back.

A good method is to carry a wire dog-grooming mitt and hold it up to protect yourself. When the horse's muzzle makes contact with the wire, he receives a sharp prick. This means that he associates nipping with discomfort and may well stop. It also seems, to the horse, less like aggression on your part than self-punishment on his and is often a successful remedy – when combined with better management.

## Eating straw bedding

Horses do this from hunger, lack of roughage and bulk, boredom or, occasionally, greed. Almost always giving a larger ration of hay stops it. You may need to balance the food intake by giving fewer concentrates, particularly with native ponies which easily get fat. Do make sure the hay is good quality: feeding poor-quality hay is likely to make the problem even worse.

Most animals nibble at fresh straw but, if large amounts are disappearing, it's nearly always when they have run out of hay, especially during the night. Changing to inedible bedding *does* stop the habit but leaves the root cause unsolved. The horse will probably vent his need in some other way, such as chewing wood or his rug, or develop a vice such as crib-biting – which often stems from hunger and indigestion.

◀ ▼ **Eating bedding:** If your horse eats excessive amounts of straw bedding, make sure you are giving him enough hay as he could lack roughage. You may need to reduce his concentrate ration correspondingly.

▼ **Nipping over the door** can be due to stress or bad temper. If it's because of stress, try to let the horse out to grass more.

If it's because of bad temper, try holding a plastic curry comb or a wire dog-grooming mitt in front of your face. Instead of biting you, the horse pricks his muzzle and learns that nipping has unpleasant consequences!

# Confidence building

To teach a horse successfully, his trainer has to encourage him to get used to new experiences and gain confidence gradually. Repetition and patience are the watchwords for this, along with well-deserved rewards.

## Practice makes perfect

When a horse is being trained he has to face many new and frightening experiences. To overcome his natural fear of being caught, led and saddled up by his trainer, he has to grow accustomed to them gradually.

The horse learns by *habituation*. This means that he is repeatedly exposed to a situation, for a short period each time.

As the name suggests, habituation relies on the horse to form habits. He does this quite readily and naturally – in a situation he has come up against before, he is most likely to behave just as he did last time. As long as no harm comes to him, the horse gradually loses his fear each time he meets the situation and accepts the training.

Police horses are taught by habituation. They have to learn to remain calm when hemmed in by large crowds, and not to be startled by loud noises, such as car horns or gun shots.

## Signal training

Horses are also trained to associate a signal with an action – a leg aid with moving forward, for example. This is most effective when the horse is about to perform the action anyway. Timing is vitally important – the signal and action must come very close together. With

▼ **A police horse** must stay calm when surrounded by a large crowd of people. By putting him in this frightening situation time and again, the horse becomes familiar with the sights and sounds and gradually loses his fear.

practice, the horse acts when he is given the signal.

Rewarding the horse immediately after he has overcome his fear has much the same effect. A pleased tone of voice or a gentle pat or scratch on the neck teaches the horse to associate the situation with something pleasant.

## In the blood

Horses with some Arab or Thoroughbred ancestors usually respond more quickly to training than cold-bloods. This doesn't mean that they are more intelligent – hot-bloods have been bred to be more highly strung, and as a result they are more sensitive to their surroundings. A hot-blood often reacts to things that a cold-blooded horse might not respond to and completely ignores.

► **Being led** is a frightening experience for a horse at first, but if you train him patiently he gradually grows used to it.

**▲ Hot-blooded horses**, like this young Arab foal, are generally easier to train than most cold-bloods. This is not because they are more intelligent – hot-bloods are spirited and this makes them sensitive and responsive to the trainer's aids.

► **Your pony** will appreciate a pat when he has faced up to a frightening situation. Timing is important – to be effective the reward must be given the instant the horse performs correctly, so that he connects the pat with his action and bravery.

# Ponies under pressure

Like humans, ponies have times when situations get on top of them. Too much stress, or distress, causes them mental and physical suffering. It pays to be on the lookout for signs of overstress in your pony.

### A sorry sight

Ponies under stress look unhappy and tense. Some react by slowing down and becoming dull and hunched; others may be peculiarly fizzy. Sudden stress caused by something frightening puts a pony on his toes, with his head up, muscles tense, and his quarters underneath him ready to make a quick getaway.

If they are under frequent mental stress, ponies develop vices as an outlet for their desire to run away from whatever bothers them. Crib-biting, weaving and banging on the door use up energy created by the wish to flee.

### Stress or distress?

A little stress or pressure in a pony's life can be beneficial. When you're trying to get a pony fit, you ask him to work a little

harder each day so his body gradually adapts to the work load. His body responds to these small increases in stress by becoming fitter.

If it is too great or too sudden, however, physical stress can harm a pony's body. An unfit pony is not prepared for hard work. Asking him to complete a cross-country course, tackle a high jump, or canter up a hill could damage his health. The tendons and ligaments in his legs may be strained or torn by the physical effort, and his heart and lungs may suffer as his system is shocked by the unfamiliar work.

Stress and concussion to the bones in the legs and feet are caused by fast work on hard surfaces – on roads in particular. A long journey by trailer makes a pony constantly tense his muscles to keep his balance, especially if the driver is careless and swings the vehicle round too much, frightening his passenger.

Illness also causes physical stress. When a healthy pony catches a disease, the infection invades his body and he becomes weak.

▼ **A good canter** with a friend in a well-kept field is an effective antidote to stress. After an intensive schooling session, a horse needs to relax and stretch his legs.

## Conflicting emotions

Worry, frustration, unhappiness, uncertainty, fear or great excitement can all lead to mental stress. It can occur at the same time as physical stress – during an illness or injury, for example, when the pony feels depressed because he is unwell or in pain.

It isn't only highly strung, finely bred horses that suffer from mental stress – a shaggy native pony can feel upset and miserable in just the same way.

The causes of mental stress vary from pony to pony, depending on what he dislikes or fears and can't escape from. It is the fact that the pony can't run away from what is disturbing him that brings on the stress.

## Be considerate

It is up to you to avoid situations that cause your pony anxiety, or to help him cope with everyday events that he finds stressful. Some problems can be solved if you are considerate to your pony and follow the basic rules of pony care.

Mental stress can be the result of too

much time in the stable, especially if the pony is eating high-energy feeds. Being cooped up in a stable is an unnatural state for any animal – he needs to stretch his legs, meet other ponies and graze. The solution is within your control – exercise him daily, turn him out and keep him occupied.

Difficult work worries a pony a great deal. He wants to do what he's asked, but

▲ **Some horses refuse** to be loaded. If kind words, food and coaxing can't persuade a horse to walk up the ramp, the situation becomes seriously distressing for all concerned. If your pony is terrified of the horsebox, don't be tempted to use shouting or violence to force him in. Instead, consult an experienced handler who can spend time getting to the bottom of the pony's fears.

◄ **Demanding work** can put mental and physical stress on a pony. Refusing is a sign that the pony is worried about clearing a certain fence. Be aware of your pony's limitations, don't push him when he seems reluctant to attempt what you're asking – he may be having an off day.

becomes confused and upset when he fails. If you ask a pony to jump a fence you're not sure he can clear, for example, you may disturb him so much that he fears jumping for the rest of his life. To make sure you don't ask too much of your pony, work out his limitations by careful schooling, preferably with an instructor.

Even tack can cause upsets. Ill-fitting or dirty tack that rubs in sensitive areas makes a pony dread being saddled long before he shows physical symptoms such as sores. Too much tack, such as severe nosebands and restrictive martingales, also distresses a pony. Help him by cleaning your tack daily, checking the fit with an expert and avoiding the use of artificial aids, if possible.

## Pony phobias

It is difficult to avoid some of the events in a pony's everyday life that can cause him mental stress. Every pony has to see the vet once in a while, but if he had a

▲ **In cold weather** a warm stable can be a pony's idea of heaven. But no animal enjoys being cooped up for hours on end. Stabled ponies must be turned out and exercised daily.

►**Having his worm dose** can be a stressful experience for a horse. Talk to your pony all the time you are treating him.

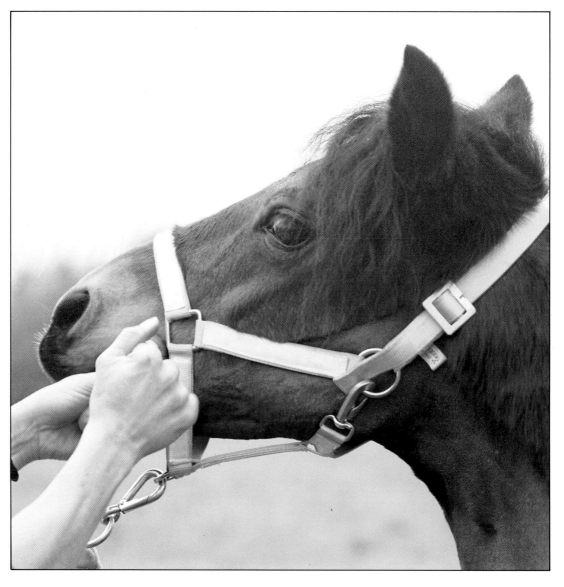

painful illness in the past, he may throw a fit every time he sees the veterinary surgeon who treated him. It may be possible to use another vet in the practice; many ponies are calmer with a woman vet if they've had a bad experience with a man, and vice versa.

There are some unfortunate ponies who are terrified of the farrier. The best way to help your pony if he dreads having new shoes is to practise the routine of picking up his feet. Tap the hoof wall with your pick to imitate the work of the farrier and make a fuss of the pony whenever he co-operates. Do your best to find a kind and understanding farrier who is patient with the nervous pony and prepared to take time reassuring him.

If your pony is difficult to transport, be patient and stay calm. Consult an expert trainer who employs a soothing, rather than a violent, technique to load horses. Sometimes a nervous pony will follow his confident field-mate into the box.

## Steps against stress

Although stress can't be avoided altogether, there are sensible steps you can take to prevent your pony being harmed by mental and physical pressure.
● Get your pony fit for strenuous work gradually, with plenty of road and hill work. Don't work him harder than his general state of fitness allows, or he may injure himself and come to associate hard work with pain and fear.
● Don't feed your pony too many concentrates.
● Make sure your pony is turned out with other, friendly ponies as often as possible. If he is bullied, separate him from the culprits.
● Don't play hectic pop music or droning chat shows on the stable radio — ponies prefer soothing classical music.
● Never lose your temper when handling or schooling your pony. Upsetting him causes distress and resentment.

▼ **Showgrounds** can make a pony go to pieces if he isn't used to the noise and bustle. Keep him as calm as possible by making sure he can relax in a quiet area in between classes.

# From stable to field or pasture

**THE FIELD**
Any field used for ponies who are out all the time should be well sheltered, preferably with a good shed, and have a reliable, clean water supply.

▼ **One of the golden rules** of horse management is to make *all* changes gradually. Take him to the field in his halter and let him graze in-hand for about 10 minutes a day for the first few days.

Changing your management system from stabling to grass may be something you do on purpose, to give your pony a holiday or a freer lifestyle. On the other hand, it may be forced on you – perhaps you lose access to the stables you use. Whatever the reason, it is important that you do it properly so the change isn't too much of a shock to the pony's system.

## The ideal way

If you have a choice, make the change over about three weeks in late spring or summer when the weather is warm. Most problems are caused by suddenly exposing the pony to cold weather after he's used to a comparatively warm stable.

The top stable door should normally be left open all the time. If you haven't done this, start as soon as you know he must be moved. Stop body brushing the pony to let natural grease build up in his coat and give some protection against the weather.

If the pony has been fed entirely on concentrates, roots and hay with no grass, start grazing him in-hand for ten minutes a day. Increase the time until, by the end of a week, he is grazing for about 30 minutes daily. At the same time start reducing his concentrates so that, after a week, he's on about three quarters of his normal ration. He should still have all the hay and water he wants. Roots, however, can now be cut down or out as he is eating grass.

## The second week

During the second week, continue to reduce his concentrates until he's on about half his full stabled ration. Keep an eye on the weather as you should also start reducing clothing. If, for example, he's been wearing a rug and two blankets, take one off now, at least during the day. If it continues mild, leave it off at night, too. By the end of the second week, he should be managing with a rug and one blanket, even if he's hunter clipped.

This second week, start turning him out instead of grazing in-hand. Ideally, give him some breakfast so he ➤

◄ **Spring or summer** is the best time to turn a pony out to grass, when it's warm enough for his coat to dry quickly even after a soaking!

▼ **Stop body brushing** the pony once you know you are turning him out. He needs natural grease to protect his coat from wind and rain. But keep picking out hooves daily, dandy brushing mud and stable stains (dried-on droppings) and tidying the mane and tail. Continue to sponge eyes, nostrils, sheath or udder and dock daily, as usual.

## EXERCISE

Many people keep ponies out all the time, not just for a rest. Your pony's exercise can be what you want it to be. If he's going out for a break, gradually reduce his ridden exercise to none by the end of the second or third week.

If the change is not for a holiday, however, keep riding and working him as normal. Remember, though, that he may need his usual supply of concentrates when out, particularly if the field is quite bare and he works hard. If the grass is very poor, he may also need hay.

Always reduce concentrates *before* reducing work.

► **A New Zealand rug** is essential for an outdoor pony who is used to being stabled. As soon as you know you are changing his routine, beg, buy or borrow as good a New Zealand rug as you can find. Ideally, have two, made of easily laundered synthetic materials, so you can always use a dry one.

won't gobble the grass. Turn him free in a small paddock where he can't gather too much speed with the joy of being free.

If you can put a quiet friend with him, this helps greatly. At least put him where he can see other horses, so he doesn't jump out looking for them and possibly hurt himself. Leave him out for about an hour on the first day, increasing to two hours daily by the end of the second week.

Assuming the weather is still mild, when the pony comes in he should manage with just his top rug (no blankets), and a concentrate ration of about a quarter of his full stabled ration.

Even if the weather turns chilly, *continue* to turn him out. Put him in a New Zealand rug and, if he feels a bit cold, increase the concentrates a little to compensate. You can tell if he's cold. He'll probably mope by the gate (although he may do this anyway if he has no company). His coat may seem to stare – standing on end in an effort to trap more insulating warm air next to the skin – and his loins, ears and flanks will feel cold. If he's really cold, he may well shiver, but he shouldn't in summer.

## The third and fourth weeks

If all continues to plan, during the third week just put on his stable rug at night. Increase his turn-out time to half a day, but continue with the New Zealand rug and concentrates if it is a little chilly. By the end of the third week, he should be out all day, have no clothing and very few concentrates. Always, however, continue with the basic grooming. Give him *ad lib* hay and water when he's in at night and keep an eye on the weather and how he's reacting to it.

By the start of the fourth week, you should be able to turn him out all the time. Be prepared to keep using the New Zealand rug and feeding concentrates if the weather becomes chilly. Otherwise, dispense with the rug altogether, and only give hard feed if you're working him. The task is now complete.

## Emergency changes

Sometimes, you have to leave your stabling at short notice. Most stables give you a week's notice and, although the gradual system is not possible, you can still help the pony to adapt.

Start at once by leaving the top stable

door open, removing one blanket, slightly reducing concentrates and grazing in-hand for half an hour. Introduce into the pony's feed dried grass meal and soaked sugar beet pulp to help his digestive system adjust. Stop body brushing at once.

If the weather is cold, never mind! Just put on a stable rug with his New Zealand rug on top for extra warmth, but try to ensure adequate changes of clothing. By having two stable rugs and two New Zealands, you can keep a clean, dry set always ready. This helps greatly to conserve body warmth, which is half your battle.

By the end of the week, have the pony out grazing all day and on about half of his stabled concentrate ration. Gradually add the dried grass meal and soaked sugar beet so the total weight of his 'bucket' feeds is the same. Slowly reduce the bucket feeds when he's out all the time but keep on with a full hay ration – he'll only eat what he needs.

Do contact your vet if the pony has unusual diarrhoea or seems at all unwell. Your instructor, too, is usually a source of expert help in an emergency.

## Golden rules for turning a stabled pony out

● Make all changes as gradual as possible. In an extreme case (a fully stabled, hunter-clipped pony), it could take up to four weeks to make the change — and that's if the weather remains mild.

● Aim to acclimatize the pony without making him feel *too* cold or giving him an upset tummy. Keep clothing handy and be prepared to use it, rather than stopping turning him out once you've started.

● Don't give the pony 'one more clip to look good' before turning him out. He needs all the hair he can get! If you know you're going to winter him out, don't clip him in the autumn at all.

● Look for a sheltered field with a reasonable grass supply, a constant, clean water supply and a friendly companion, to give him the best possible chance of adjusting happily.

● Try to keep *some* grass always in your pony's diet. Then, if you are faced with a sudden loss of stabling and have to make a quick change, it isn't too much of a shock to his digestive system.

● Keep a keen eye on his behaviour and condition, and on the weather. Don't hesitate to ask advice from your vet or instructor if you are at all worried about the pony.

● Keep up to date with what accommodation is available in your area. Ask horsy friends, your local riding or Pony Club, and your instructor, and check advertisements in your local paper, so you have a good idea where to go for alternative stabling.

**A stabled horse** may take off with the joy of freedom when first let out, so put him in a small paddock for safety.

# Rewards and bribes

**! DANGER –**
**! CORRUPTION!**

Don't overdo the titbits or the horse may stop looking upon them as a treat and a reward for work done well, and demand them as his right.

Instead of helping to make him good, too many snacks may make him naughty and bad-mannered. He may start poking around in pockets and even tearing clothing to find what he wants. More seriously, he may chase strangers in the field, threatening to bite or kick if they do not give him food.

▼ **The natural** herd instinct of the horse can be a useful training tool – a nervous horse will follow a lead from another over a jump or past an obstacle.

Rewarding a horse is the best way to show he has performed well and, as such, is useful in training. Bribery, too, can be used positively – to help overcome fear of a frightening situation.

## Training with kindness

By nature horses are timid animals whose instinct is to run away from danger. This explains why horses sometimes show fear when you ask them to do something for the first time: 'Will I be trapped if I enter this dark box of a stable?' 'What is lurking in this water she wants me to wade through?'.

If they are to become confident and courageous, horses need to be trained with a mixture of kindness, understanding and firmness. You have to think about how the horse's mind works, so that you know whether hesitation or a show of fear is genuine or not.

Horses like to please humans and, when rewarded for overcoming their fear, or for doing well, come to link the action with pleasure.

## Giving praise

There are various methods of giving praise, which depend on the work done and the individual horse. Praise such as 'good' and 'well done' in a pleased tone of voice is often enough to make the horse feel rewarded.

Work needing concentration can be rewarded with a few moments on a long rein, letting the pony stretch his neck and relax. For a strenuous performance like a gymkhana event or jumping a course, dismount and allow the pony to

▼ **Titbits** are commonly used as a bribe when catching a difficult or timid pony – his greed conquers all resistance!

relax completely and enjoy a titbit.

Whenever the pony does well in small things, he may appreciate a gentle pat or scratch on the neck. This reminds him of his mother's nuzzling when he was a foal. All praise should be given immediately after the event or the horse will not realize what it is for.

## Bribing a horse

Although horses do not reason in the same way as humans do, they are intelligent and sensitive and have excellent memories. They can be persuaded to do most things required of them by learning to associate the situation they fear with something pleasant – like the company of other horses or going home.

The instinct of safety in numbers can be useful. A nervous horse will often follow others through water, over a jump or past a 'strange' obstacle like a tractor and so gain the courage to do it by himself in future.

A horse also passes an obstacle he is unsure of more readily if going toward the stable. And you may notice when jumping a course that the pony takes the fences facing toward home with unexpected verve!

► **Reward good work** at once, so the pony associates what he has just done with the praise.

▼ **Entering a van** can be very frightening. The space is small and the floor feels unsafe. The presence of other ponies and the offer of food helps ponies overcome their fear.

PART FIVE

# QUESTIONS
# ANSWERED

# Bad behaviour

## Q

My pony is all right when we go out for a ride, but as soon as we start for home she gets silly. She shies at anything and jogs, and when we get to the cantering places she wants to gallop. What can I do about this?

## A

This is a difficult problem to deal with. It is quite common for ponies to perk up when they're on their way home, even after quite long rides, but in your pony's case it has become plain naughtiness.

You have to be very firm with her and make her walk all the way home until she learns to go quietly. Every time she jogs, quietly bring her back to walk and praise her when she does as you ask. Keep her walking slowly and calmly, and keep the rein contact light – don't pull or you'll just end up in a tug-of-war contest.

You might also try turning her away from home again as soon as she is naughty, so that she learns she won't get home until she is good. If you can, vary the places you canter – even on the ride out – so it's your decision where to canter and not hers. And if you are able to, vary your route so you don't always go the same way home.

If your normal routine is to feed her soon after you get home from a ride, she may be anxious for her meal, so change the feeding time.

## Q

My pony is usually very good, but he always tries to kick the blacksmith when he is being shod. How can I stop him doing this?

## A

One short-term answer is to pull down hard on his tail, which makes it difficult for him to kick.

It may be that he doesn't like that blacksmith (perhaps he had a bad experience with him), in which case find another, but warn the new one that he should allow plenty of time to do the job gently. Then go away and let the blacksmith deal with it on his own. If you are nervous, your pony will sense it and won't relax.

When you buy a pony, you should take great care to make sure you are getting exactly what you want – with no hidden extras!

## Buying a pony

What do you do when the pony you've just bought turns out to be a problem? Your first thought might be to return him to the seller and ask for your money back. You must not leave it too long to do this. Behaviour problems should become obvious within a month, or the sellers could say you caused the problem yourself – either through bad riding or bad management.

Whether you can return the pony at all depends on what was written on the warranty when you bought him. If the sellers lied to you in writing about the pony's vices, you can return him. If they didn't mention a fault and you didn't ask, it is a case of 'Buyer Beware' and you are stuck with the pony.

Otherwise you have the options of sorting the problem out yourself, or admitting you have made a mistake and selling the pony on. Hard though this may sound, it is better than keeping a pony you can't ride.

## Solving the problem

There are some behaviour problems you can deal with yourself, especially with professional help. Naughtiness and

vices are often the result of:

● **Bad riding:** It could be that you are not being firm and clear enough with your pony. Horses often take advantage of riders who are unsure of themselves, and test the rider to see how much they can get away with.

● **Insufficient schooling:** If your pony has not been properly schooled, or has never been schooled at all, he may genuinely misunderstand what it is you are asking him to do. He has not learned to be obedient to a rider's instructions, such as moving forward from the leg aid without resistance. If this is the case, you need professional help to work out a schooling programme for your pony.

● **Pain:** Your pony may be playing up because something is hurting him. Badly fitting or worn tack causes discomfort, and may make the pony buck or throw his head about. Or the pony may have a health problem, such as painful teeth or a sore back, which is making him misbehave.

● **Incorrect feeding:** If a pony has excess energy, it could be that you are giving him too much concentrated feed for the amount of work he is asked to carry out.

▼ **The presence of other ponies** often encourages a nervous or nappy pony and helps him to overcome his fears.

Every time we stop my pony wants to eat. He pulls at the reins and I fall off. What can I do?

Two things. The first is to have some riding lessons! If your seat is so insecure that this makes you fall off, you shouldn't be out on your own.

The second is to be prepared for it and not let him put his head down. When you are going to stop, take an extra firm hold on the reins and brace yourself in the saddle. If he tries to reach down, pull back sharply, say 'NO!' loudly and make him walk on again.

You could also try fitting some 'grass reins' on your pony. Tie a length of binder twine to each bit ring; pass the twine up through the browband loops and attach the other end to the D-rings on each side of the saddle. Make them short enough to stop him putting his head down, but not so tight that they pull his head in.

My pony keeps stopping when I'm riding him, he walks backward and won't go any further. How can I stop him doing it?

This behaviour is called 'napping' or 'jibbing', and can be very frustrating for the rider – often the tougher you get with the pony the more he naps, so hitting him can make it worse. Try circling him a few times so he temporarily loses his sense of direction, and then immediately ride him forward. And if he starts to go backward, turn him round and make him back the way you want him to go for a few paces.

There are several possible reasons why he might have developed this behaviour. He may be genuinely frightened of something and trying to get away, so think about where he does it – is it always in the same place, or always where he sees the same object (like a farmyard or a lawn-mower, for instance)? If this is the case you need some friends on ponies to come with you and give him courage – especially if you have recently bought the pony and the area is strange to him.

If the cause isn't fright, it could be that he is in pain – his back or mouth may be hurting him, for instance – so have him and his tack thoroughly checked. Or it could be that you are not riding strongly enough and he is taking advantage of you. In this case you should go to a professional instructor for help with your riding and advice on schooling your pony.

# Nervousness

## Q

At the local riding school where I work one of the horses constantly bites my friend and appears to be nervous when she is near him. The same horse is perfectly calm with me. Why do you think this is?

## A

It sounds as if your friend has either hurt or upset this horse at some time, or is frightened of him. In the first instance, the horse remembers that she hurt him and is napping in self-defence or anticipation of further distress. However, it usually takes more than one incident to produce this behaviour. In the second instance, the horse can sense she is frightened and feels he has the upper hand!

In either case, your friend should handle the horse carefully but confidently, talking reassuringly to him but saying a firm 'no' when he tries to nip. If the habit persists the horse must be tied up before she handles him. She should also talk the problem over with one of the instructors at the school, who knows the pony.

---

## Q

I have been schooling my pony for a long time and recently I started taking him to shows. Unfortunately, every time we arrive he behaves very badly and refuses to jump, although he pops over fences happily at home. What can I do?

## A

It could be that your pony realizes that if he doesn't jump at shows you won't persist as you might do during a schooling session at home. He may be upset by the exciting atmosphere of a show or perhaps he might have had an unpleasant experience in a show ring, and now thinks it's going to happen again.

Try taking him to a few shows without jumping. Enter showing classes on the flat, or ride him round near the jumps, speaking soothingly to him. When he is really calm, try beginners' jumping classes at local club meetings which involve only small jumps.

Be sure you practise at home over brightly painted jumps similar to those you'll meet in the ring so he becomes used to them. However, over-jumping can easily sicken the pony and cause refusals. If you are having problems, rest him from jumping for a few weeks, then try again under expert supervision. Also, try asking your instructor or an experienced friend to jump him at shows, then they can help you assess what his exact problem is.

Just like humans, some horses and ponies are more nervous and highly strung than others. Before you can overcome any problems, you need to recognize the signs and understand the causes of excitable behaviour.

## The signs and causes

Sometimes nervousness shows itself by extreme alertness. The pony is unreasonably spooky and tosses his head. If you are riding, you may also sense the pony trembling. The muscles, especially on his neck, feel tense and hard. When you look at him, a nervous pony's expression is often one of uncertainty or even fear – wide eyes, flared nostrils – and he may snort or spin round to try to run away. A pony that is really terrified stands rooted to the spot.

Nervousness can be inherited or caused by careless handling in the past. Bad stable management is also a culprit – stabling two enemies next to one another, for instance, quickly creates tension. And feeding too many concen-

trates combined with too little exercise is a significant cause.

All foods produce poisonous waste products in the body, but concentrates make many more than bulk foods. These poisons cause unnatural sensitivity and nervousness.

## Overcoming the problem

An experienced, patient trainer can overcome nervousness in youngsters by showing them that there is nothing to be afraid of. He gradually gains their confidence. Regulating the diet, and keeping the pony in favourable conditions, also helps him to remain calm.

Most horses want leadership and in the absence of the stallion or lead mare of a herd, they look to humans to supply it. Confident, calm humans help create confident, calm horses.

▼ **Contented horses** tend to pass their calm attitude to life on to their foals. A nervous youngster, however, needs sympathetic handling to build his confidence.

**Q**

I bought my pony when he was a five year old. Every time we ride near water he becomes frightened. Can you suggest what causes this and what cure there is?

**A**

Some ponies don't like getting wet, and others are afraid of the sound of rushing water. It's possible your pony had an unpleasant experience with water before you bought him. In this case, it could be very difficult to cure completely. Try taking him out with a horse who doesn't mind water, keeping the calm one between your pony and the water at first. Next, let your pony see other horses standing in water (with their riders chatting as if nothing was unusual, but staying alert). Calm your pony at the same time. When he is more confident, try persuading him to follow another into water. Alternatively, ask a more competent rider to swap ponies until yours improves. *Never* force your pony.

**Q**

My horse is very nervous if I ride out alone and he always naps when we pass the field where his companions are turned out. He is perfectly happy when a group of us ride out together. What can I do about this?

**A**

Horses are herd animals and feel safest in a crowd. Few like being isolated but they must learn to work alone and take their lead from you. You must be calm, strong and persistent.

If your horse is very unsettled, try riding out with just one other horse for a while on quiet roads. Over the days and weeks, ride farther and farther apart, asking one horse to pass the other and so on, then try coming home separate ways. Your horse will probably be more concerned about reaching home than playing up! If he continues to fidget, ask an expert rider to hack him out on his own until he is used to working alone. Give him plenty of exercise and freedom and not too many concentrates.

# Grooming and sensitivity

Grooming is a task that should be done every day and is important to a pony's well-being and appearance. However, not all ponies enjoy the process.

### The gentle touch

Those who have been handled gently but firmly from a young age give little trouble. It is horses who have been roughly treated or allowed to get away with silly behaviour who cause problems. These may include headshyness, kicking and biting.

Some horses refuse to stand still even when they are tied up: they may try to corner their handlers behind them to avoid being groomed.

Plenty of horses have sensitive skin, in particular hot-bloods. Their coats don't give much protection from brush bristles, especially from dandy or water brushes. Even a properly kept body brush has a slightly scratchy effect on the skin, particularly on a summer coat or clipped winter coat. Plastic-toothed curry combs are quite harsh unless used considerately.

Ponies are most sensitive in those areas where the skin is thinnest – under the belly, inside the legs and around the sheath/udder and dock. The head is another touchy area.

The eyes, ears, muzzle and 'feeler' hairs are all sensitive, too.

### Handle with care

If your pony objects to a particular area being groomed, be patient and try to achieve a little more each time.

First, try stroking him with your hands, then with a stable rubber. Graduate to a cactus cloth and increase the pressure over the days or weeks. Finally, move on to proper brushes. He's almost certain to accept your touch once he knows you won't hurt him.

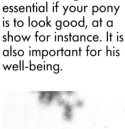

▼ **Grooming** is essential if your pony is to look good, at a show for instance. It is also important for his well-being.

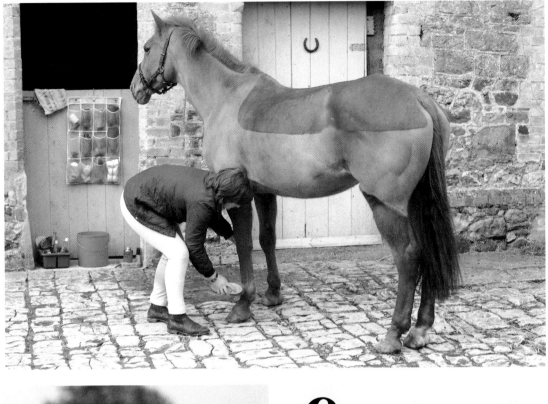

◄ **When you groom a pony** take special care around any bony areas. Be particularly gentle where his coat is thinnest after clipping.

# Q

My pony flinches and jogs about during grooming, sometimes snatching at me with a nasty face. How can I stop him doing this?

# A

It sounds very much as though your pony is ticklish and you are grooming him too roughly. Never scrub at him, particularly with a dandy brush or plastic curry comb, and *never* use a metal curry comb on him. Be much more gentle with him and talk soothingly. Never mind if you don't truly clean him at first. It is more important to regain his trust and reassure him that you aren't going to be rough in the future.

# Q

My pony lets me groom him everywhere except his head. He sticks his nose up in the air where I can't reach. What can I do?

# A

Ask an experienced handler to help if the pony is nervous. First, tie the pony up with just the headpiece of the headcollar (halter) round his neck, to keep him from throwing his head up.

Then put away your brushes and try to 'groom' him using your *hands* only.

Start with his neck and then go under his jaw, on to the sides of his face and down the front of it. Avoid his ears, eyes and muzzle, until you have gained his trust.

While you are stroking him with one hand, give the pony his favourite titbit with the other hand so he comes to associate head-grooming with a special treat.

Gradually move on to a stable rubber and finally to a body brush. Always be careful not to knock the pony. Praise him when he is good.

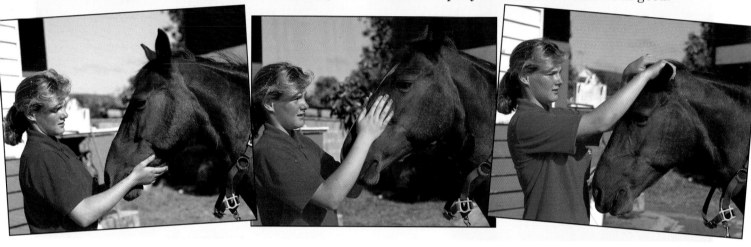

# Q

One of the ponies at our local riding school has a very greasy coat and it's hard to get him sleek and clean. Another of the ponies in the yard has a dry, dull coat which never looks good. How can we improve them?

# A

Like people, some ponies have naturally oily skin and others dry skin. Feeding has a great deal to do with skin and coat condition. Ask a vet to check the ponies' diets for oil/fat content and advise you how to adjust them accordingly. The pony with greasy skin would benefit from a weekly or fortnightly shampoo. The dry-skinned one could benefit from having linseed oil added to his food – about 10ml (a tablespoonful) every day.

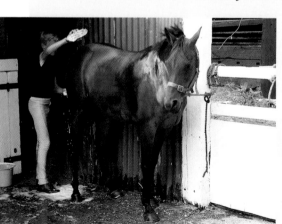

# Q

What can I do with a pony who constantly walks around, avoiding me when I try to groom him?

# A

Tie him up! Use a strong headcollar and tie him up with his nose about 15cm (6in) from a wall or fence, in case he tries to bite you. If he still jigs about or swings his quarters around, be patient. Talk soothingly to him and give him a hay net to help calm him down. Remember that if he's avoiding being groomed it is because he doesn't like it. Be gentle, particularly with coarser brushes. Don't knock any bony parts and be especially careful around sensitive areas.

▼ **A shiny coat and well-groomed appearance** are easy to achieve if you have a trusting relationship with your horse.

# Q

My pony loses clumps of hair from his mane and tail when I groom him, so that they have become quite thin. Why is this and how can I prevent it happening?

# A

Your pony could have a skin disorder or parasite infestation, so ask a vet to check him over.

Alternatively hair loss could be the result of incorrect grooming. If you use a dandy brush you are likely to pull out too much hair. It is best to use a shorter-bristled brush such as a water or body brush and be very gentle. Some hair is bound to come out naturally. Ponies shed more mane and tail hair in spring and autumn, but you shouldn't notice much difference.

Always unpick knots and tangles with your *fingers*, not the brush. Start at the bottom of the hairs and work upward or you'll make the tangles worse. Never pull the hair! Don't use a mane comb for grooming – it is meant only for trimming.

# Q

A pony I look after has mud fever on his legs and belly and a rash on his back. How do I groom him?

# A

You *don't* groom the diseased areas – partly because it causes pain and partly because it can spread the disease to healthy skin. Treat the diseased areas as directed by your vet and groom other areas normally.

# Stallions, geldings, mares

Most animals reproduce by mating. With horses, the mating season runs from spring through to the end of summer. At this time, stallions (males capable of siring a foal) and mares (females capable of having a foal) are affected by hormones (chemical substances), which encourage mating.

## Geldings

A gelding is a male who has been castrated so that he cannot sire a foal.

**Q**

I have seen a lovely eight-year-old stallion I would like to buy. Could I have him gelded?

**A**

Yes, you could, although eight is rather late to geld a stallion, and you should discuss the matter with your veterinarian and instructor.

With older horses, it often takes several months, even a year or more, for their minds and bodies to become accustomed to being a gelding instead of a stallion. However, the sexual instincts are curbed, they are unable to sire a foal, and they show less interest toward in-season mares. Most do quieten down eventually and become successful riding horses.

**Q**

My gelding behaves badly around mares and acts like a stallion. Can you suggest why? I have been told he may be a rig, but I'm not sure what this is.

**A**

If he acts like a stallion he could be a rig. This is a male horse or pony who has not been properly gelded. Only one testicle has been removed and the other has remained up in the abdomen, never having dropped down between his hindlegs as normal. This means that he behaves like a stallion and is even capable of siring a foal.

Your vet can carry out tests to check this and can also operate to remove the remaining testicle, which would make your pony a proper gelding.

Some true geldings behave badly around mares simply because they do not like females or because they are badly disciplined and poorly trained. If your vet confirms that your pony is *not* a rig, extra schooling is called for.

There are two main reasons for gelding: to make the pony easier to handle, and to prevent animals of poor type passing on their faults to their offspring.

Colts (young males) can be gelded at any time provided their testicles (the male reproductive organs that produce sperm to fertilize the mare's egg) are hanging down outside the body, between the hindlegs in the scrotal sacs. This often happens at birth but in some cases they do not drop until about 18 months of age. However, abdominal testicles can be removed under a general anaesthetic.

Most people geld their animals in the spring of their yearling year or even the autumn before. Pedigree stock, racehorses and heavy, working horses, however, are often left until it is known whether or not they are good enough to be kept as stallions for breeding.

## Stallions

Stallions are altogether more alert and fiery than geldings. Their necks are muscular and well crested. They can be very lively to ride and handle. If they are on the lookout for mares and feel the desire to mate, it can take expert and sensitive handling to hold them. For this reason most working horses are gelded to make them calmer.

Stallions can make superb rides in the right hands. They understand and respect discipline, but can become vicious if badly handled. Much, however, depends on an individual's temperament.

Only the really good males should be kept entire (as stallions). For most purposes it is kinder, and more practical, to have a stallion gelded.

Domesticated stallions lead restricted lives. They cannot normally be turned out with others as they might pester the mares and fight geldings, thinking they are rivals. So, they are often kept out alone and have no contact with others.

## Mares

Most mares are just as easy to handle as geldings except when they are in season, which occurs about every three weeks during the spring and summer. Then they may be more nervous and highly strung; more alert, but less inclined to work.

Mares can be operated on to prevent them from having foals and coming in season. But this is stressful for the mare and expensive for the owner!

▼ **Gelding a pony** generally makes him calmer and easier to handle than a stallion.

I am considering having my yearling gelded, but I am worried that it is cruel. Do horses know what is happening to them?

It would certainly be cruel to geld horses without either a general anaesthetic (which makes the pony unconscious), or a local anaesthetic (which simply deadens feeling in the area to be operated on). But, in most countries, an anaesthetic is compulsory by law, so the animal feels little or nothing.

After the operation, pain killers can be given in case the pony feels some soreness, and the wound must be watched carefully for signs of swelling and infection. Otherwise, ponies don't know exactly what has happened to them, or understand its consequences, so don't worry.

My mare becomes very difficult when she's in season. Is there anything I can do about this?

It depends on just how difficult she becomes. She may feel you are not strong enough to discipline her and she tries to get away with 'marish' behaviour. But mares in season rarely behave absolutely normally, and they need good, understanding riders. Your instructor may recommend extra schooling or stronger riding on your part.

Don't take your mare near stallions and ask other riders to keep their mounts away from her quarters. If she gets agitated, calm her by stroking and talking to her. If she goes too far, a stern 'no' should remind her of her manners – but don't hit her as this might upset her even more.

You can give mares hormones to prevent them from coming into season. Ask your vet for advice.

# Mouth matters

**Healthy teeth** and a comfortable mouth are essential if a pony is to respond to your aids when you're out riding.

To stay healthy, a pony must have a good set of teeth: incisors to bite food and premolars and molars to grind it up for digestion. The front teeth rarely cause problems, but the cheek teeth are often at the root of ill health and riding problems.

## Teething troubles

Although you can only see the pony's first cheek teeth when you put the bit in his mouth, you should be able to tell if anything is wrong by certain signs:
● Reluctance to eat although the pony may still be interested in his food.
● Loss of condition.
● Undigested food in the droppings.
● Quidding – dropping half-chewed pieces of food from the mouth.

Tooth problems often go hand in hand with equitation faults, such as reluctance to take the bit or hanging to one side. If your pony is not responding normally to your aids ask your vet to examine his mouth.

Ponies sometimes have an 'extra' tooth just in front of the upper premolars and molars, known as a 'wolf tooth'. Wolf teeth can have sharp points. Sometimes they don't come through the gums but remain as a gum swelling. This may be knocked by the bit.

## Grinding surfaces

The cheek teeth are worn down by grinding. But, unlike human teeth, they continue to grow throughout the horse's life to compensate for the wear. Premolars and molars, however, wear unevenly and sharp points often develop which cut the cheeks or tongue. So rasping is necessary from time to time to level out the surfaces.

In old horses, teeth often come out of alignment and wear very unevenly. They may even fall out. In this case, the tooth above or below is no longer worn down, but becomes long and sharp unless it is rasped frequently. Old ponies can become thin if their cheek teeth are no longer able to grind their food properly, or if they cause pain.

## Baby teeth

Like children, foals are born with a set of temporary 'baby' teeth. They are replaced by permanent ones between the ages of two and five years. 'Teething' ponies need more frequent dental attention as the baby teeth are sharp.

Call your vet if you suspect any tooth problems. But, depending on the alignment of your pony's teeth, you should have them inspected at least once a year even if they are trouble free. Try to have them rasped at the same time as booster vaccinations are given – that way both jobs are remembered.

If your pony is young (under five) or old (over 20) his teeth should be checked twice a year. An old pony with bad teeth may need them rasped every 2-3 months to stop him losing condition. Not all horses' teeth are perfectly aligned; they may need attention every 6 months.

▲ **A horse must eat** properly if he is to stay in condition. Healthy teeth ensure that a pony can chew his food ready for digestion.

## Diagram of a newly formed incisor tooth

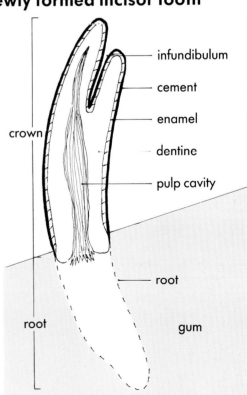

The tooth can be divided into two sections, the crown and the root.

The crown is the part which appears above the gum and it consists of three layers: the cement, the enamel and the dentine. The blood supply reaches the tooth via the pulp cavity. The root anchors the tooth firmly in the gum.

The infundibulum is present in the teeth of young horses, but gradually disappears as the tooth wears down.

- infundibulum
- cement
- enamel
- dentine
- pulp cavity
- root

crown

root    gum

**Q**

My sister and I were looking at a pony at a sale. Someone advised us not to buy her because she had a 'parrot mouth'. What does this mean?

**A**

When the front teeth in the pony's upper jaw are in front of those in its lower jaw, the condition is called 'parrot mouth'. It is also known as an 'over-shot' jaw.

A horse is born with this condition and, unfortunately, nothing can be done about it. If the teeth are only slightly out of alignment the animal may be able to eat normally, but if there is a gap between them, it can make feeding difficult. So if a parrot-mouthed pony is turned out he could become thin, and he may need extra concentrates to stay in good condition. The teeth do not wear evenly and may need continual dental attention.

If you are thinking of breeding horses, a parrot-mouthed animal is *not* a good choice as the condition is hereditary.

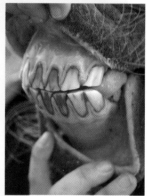

▲ **A parrot mouth is** when the pony's upper front teeth are out of alignment with the bottom front ones. The teeth do not wear down and need constant attention.

► **Well-aligned teeth** are worn down evenly with the action of grinding the food.

**Q**

Do horses get toothache?

**A**

If a pony has a problem, such as an abscess, involving a tooth *root*, he can certainly be very sorry for himself. However, his teeth are longer than a human's teeth, and the crown (the part of the tooth you can see) is a long way from the nerves in the tooth root. So problems in the crown don't appear to cause discomfort.

Horses do suffer from tooth decay, but it is not common. Although they like sweet treats, they don't eat them continually!

Old horses are the most likely to have a decayed tooth, as particles of food can be trapped in crevices for long periods. Rasping the teeth helps to prevent this. Luckily, the teeth keep growing and new tooth from below can replace the decayed portion. The tremendous force with which horses grind their teeth together means that fillings would not remain intact for very long.

▲ **Beware**, too many sweets might cause tooth decay!

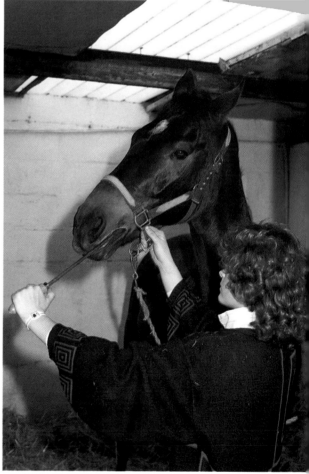

▲ **Rasping** evens out the sharp points of a horse's teeth, which are a result of their constant growth.

When I bought my pony I noticed that he has 'wolf teeth' on both sides of his upper jaw. Although they are not causing any trouble, I have been told that they should be removed. Is this correct?

If wolf teeth are making the pony difficult for you to ride or are causing him discomfort, they should certainly be removed.

Wolf teeth usually have shallow roots and can be taken out fairly easily, under a local anaesthetic. Sometimes they are deeply embedded into the jaw bone and may require an operation, under general anaesthetic, to remove them. In either case, the pony should be rested for 4-6 weeks afterwards, which gives his gums a chance to heal.

However, it is *not* necessary to remove the pony's wolf teeth unless they are giving him trouble.

Our three-year-old filly has a hard, pink swelling on the roof of her mouth, just behind her front teeth. Is this anything to do with her teeth?

This condition is known as *lampas*. The hard palate (which forms the roof of the mouth) swells, usually as a result of teething in young horses. However, it can sometimes appear in older horses for no apparent reason.

Lampas does not require any treatment, as it clears up on its own. However, feed your filly a softer diet for a while, to prevent any pain. Soak her hay and mix water with pony nuts to make a sort of gruel.

My pony is reluctant to take the bit when I am riding him. Could this be due to tooth trouble?

Reluctance to take the bit is often associated with a dental problem. If there is a wolf tooth beneath the gums, pressure from the bit causes pain on the area. The action of the bit may also pull the cheeks or tongue against sharp edges of the cheek teeth, causing cuts or ulcers in the mouth. Call your vet and ask him to examine your pony. In most cases, rasping the sharp points quickly solves the problem.

**On examination** a vet can quickly tell if a horse's teeth are causing problems.

My pony has a hard swelling on the side of his face below his left eye. The vet says that this is a tooth root abscess. Is this serious?

Abscesses in tooth roots are quite common. They can be painful for the pony and are quite difficult to treat. The roots of some of the upper cheek teeth lie inside the sinuses. This means that pus coming from an abscess here, may appear at the nostrils. An infected tooth root can cause swelling in the jaw bone.

Although antibiotics usually clear up the infection, the swelling often remains. In some cases, antibiotics are not enough and the tooth needs to be removed, allowing the abscess to drain. After this operation the pony's mouth is sore and he is reluctant to eat for a few days, but does make a full recovery.

# Food for thought

In the pony's digestive system there are micro-organisms which help him digest his food. If these are upset, harmful bacteria can take over and cause problems for the pony.

## Keeping the balance

To maintain the balance of 'helpful' micro-organisms in the gut, follow these 'rules'.

**Feed little and often** – at least 2-3 feeds a day – or let the pony have several periods of grazing, with no long gaps between them.

**Feed a little of each ingredient** with each meal, not oats for breakfast, nuts for lunch and so on.

**Feed plenty of bulk.**

**Make any changes in feeding gradually** – whether going on to a new type of food or a new variety of the same food. Introduce any new feed by building it up

over a 7-21 day period, and where possible, by mixing new with old for at least 7 days.

## Making the change
Changing a pony from being kept in or out should also be done gradually. If this is not possible, continue to give hay or straw for 1-3 weeks after turning out, or cut and feed fresh grass daily if the pony is brought in.

Such care gives the horse's digestion a chance to adjust to the new feed and use it efficiently. His system has time to alter its output of different enzymes (chemicals that help the breakdown of food and digestion), as some foodstuffs need more than others.

Food should be clean and dust free to avoid allergies, either in the lungs or on the skin. Some moulds produce poisons which can be very dangerous for ponies.

▼ It is most natural for ponies to graze on and off all day. Their digestive systems are designed to cope with frequent, small amounts of food.

# Q

My pony keeps shaking his head when I ride him and when he eats hard food he drops it out of his mouth. Why is this and how can I prevent it?

# A

Dropping food from the mouth like this is called 'quidding'. Your pony almost certainly has problems with his teeth. They may have sharp edges which are cutting into his cheeks, or he may have an abscess. Call your vet and have your pony checked. Once the problem is overcome, continue to have his teeth checked regularly, as advised by the vet.

# Q

I've noticed that the ponies in a field near my home paw at a bank and seem to lick or eat the soil. The grass in the field looks green so why do they do it?

# A

The ponies are probably craving a particular mineral which they are lacking. It is quite likely that this is salt, and that there is a salty patch of earth in the bank. The owner should supply a salt lick, as well as adding salt to any concentrated feed if the ponies are in hard work.

If it isn't salt, the ponies could be short of other minerals, trace elements, or fibre if the grass is very lush. In the last instance, the soil may contain a special type of clay which swells up and acts as a fibre substitute (you can even buy such a product – sodium montmerrillonite). Ponies with a fibre deficiency also strip bark off trees. They should have the mineral levels in their diets checked and be given plenty of bulk feeds.

The pony must have access to clean, fresh water to prevent him from dehydrating. In the stable, water becomes flat and unpalatable so replace it often. Don't just top it up. In the field, check the trough regularly for debris.

Dehydration is a common cause of colic in winter, so be prepared to break ice 2-3 times a day in cold weather.

## Vet check

Proper parasite control, as advised by your vet, is essential in keeping your pony worm and parasite free. This allows him to take the full value from his food. It also prevents migrating worm larvae from causing colic.

Have your pony's teeth checked every six months if he is very young or very old, and yearly if he is somewhere in between. More regular rasping may be necessary if the teeth are badly aligned.

▼ **Make sure a pony has access to clean, fresh water** at all times of the day. Check the trough daily to see that it is filling up properly, and remove any fallen leaves or debris that collect in it.

▲ **Any changes to a pony's diet** should be carried out *gradually*. If he is recently turned out, continue to give him hay for a few weeks. This allows his digestive system to adjust steadily to the *new* food.

# Q

My pony is greedy and bolts his food. I don't think this is very good for him, but how can I prevent it?

# A

No, it isn't good for him to bolt his food as he cannot digest it properly and could get colic or other digestive upsets.

First, make the feed one that he *has* to chew, by adding chaff or molassed chaff, and perhaps using extruded (minced) cereals. Second, if you have a long manger, spread the feed out, and place a few large, flat stones along its length so the horse has to eat round them. Make sure you clean both the manger and the stones regularly.

# Q

My pony had to have antibiotics six months ago and, since then, his droppings have been rather loose. Is this connected with his feeding or digestion?

# A

The antibiotics kill some of the 'good' micro-organisms as well as the disease they are prescribed to destroy. Ask your vet about 'probiotics' (freeze-dried, 'good' micro-organisms) or sodium montmerrillonite (a fibre substitute) – both of which help to bring the gut back to normal. Also, feed your pony plenty of roughage.

# Q

My pony keeps eating his droppings. I've seen foals do the same. Why do they do it and is it bad for them?

# A

The behaviour is known as coprophagy. Foals do it to pick up digestive micro-organisms from the mother's droppings and so build up the numbers in their own digestive systems. It is quite natural but you can help by giving the foals a suitable probiotic – under guidance from the vet.

When adult horses practise coprophagy it is a sign that either their digestive micro-organisms are upset and need re-balancing or that they are deficient in protein, certain minerals or bulk. Correct feeding and a course of probiotics can help to put the pony back on the right track.

# Breathing disorders

**DID YOU KNOW?**
A horse's lungs provide a huge area for oxygen absorption, which gives them the stamina for prolonged exercise. The internal lung area (called the *alveolar surface area*) measures around 2,500 square metres (2,989 square yards). In comparison, a human has only 90-120 square metres (107-143 square yards)!

Horses and ponies are good athletes because they have an efficient respiratory (breathing) system. This supplies them with oxygen which is vital for the chemical reactions that keep them alive.

## The passage of air

Horses cannot breathe through their mouths, because they have a long *soft palate* that shuts off the airways from the back of the mouth. Instead, they breathe through the nose. Their nostrils flare, funnelling air inside. Within the nose the air passes through channels where it is warmed by blood vessels.

From the *nasal passage*, the air enters a large chamber beneath the base of the skull called the *pharynx*. Next, it passes through the *larynx,* which forms the entrance to the lower airway. The larynx is a collection of cartilages at the top of the *trachea* (wind pipe). It keeps the airway permanently open.

## The lower airways

Air passes down the trachea, which runs close to the front of the neck. At the entrance to the *lungs*, the trachea divides into two main tubes called *bronchi*. One bronchus goes to each lung. The lungs occupy the whole of the chest cavity, except for a space on the left side where the heart is.

Inside the lungs the bronchi divide and subdivide into many small tubes called *bronchioles* which eventually lead to the *alveoli* (air sacs).

## Absorbing oxygen

Muscle cells in particular require a lot of oxygen which provides the energy for repeated contraction during exercise.

When air reaches the lungs, oxygen is absorbed by the alveoli. There are millions of these air sacs and they have thin walls to help absorption, coupled with a good blood supply to transport oxygen around the body.

## Breathing

At rest, a healthy pony breathes 8-14 times a minute. Breathing in is brought about by the muscular *diaphragm* contracting, and breathing out happens when the diaphragm expands.

During exercise the breathing rate increases. Muscles pull the ribs forward and outward, expanding the chest and pulling more air into the lungs.

At the walk and trot, a horse breathes

## Diagrammatic view of the respiratory system

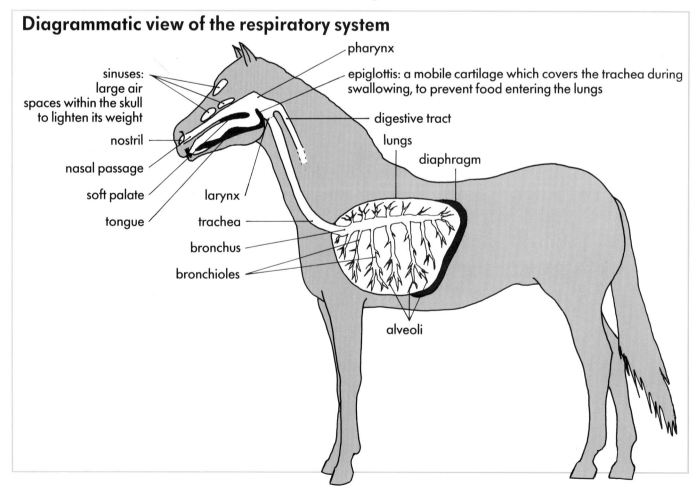

sinuses: large air spaces within the skull to lighten its weight

nostril

nasal passage

soft palate

tongue

larynx

trachea

bronchus

bronchioles

pharynx

epiglottis: a mobile cartilage which covers the trachea during swallowing, to prevent food entering the lungs

digestive tract

lungs

diaphragm

alveoli

regularly. But at faster paces it can only breathe once during each stride – breathing in when the forelegs are off the ground and going forward, and breathing out when they are on the ground.

The rate and depth of breathing are controlled by nerve impulses from the brain, in response to oxygen levels in the blood. Very rapid, shallow, noisy or distressed breathing *at rest* are signs that something is wrong. If you discover your pony breathing abnormally you should call your vet at once.

Other signs of trouble in the respiratory system are coughing, nasal discharge and swollen glands beneath the chin. If you notice any of these symptoms, call in a vet as all of them require treatment.

▼ **Most horses** are excellent athletes. Their breathing systems provide plenty of oxygen for their hard-working muscles.

# Q

Do ponies get colds or flu like humans?

# A

There are several viruses that can cause flu-like symptoms in ponies. The most common one is called Equine Herpes Virus type 1 (EHV1). It is very mild, resulting in a watery discharge from the nostrils and a slight cough for a few days.

Ponies can also suffer from equine influenza, which, like human flu, usually occurs in epidemics. It is highly infectious and is easily spread by coughing. Infected horses become quite sick, running a high temperature and going off their food. They usually have a lot of discharge from the nostrils and a cough which may last for weeks or even months.

You can protect your pony from this disease by vaccination. Ask your vet for advice.

**Vaccination** stops the spread of colds and flu where horses meet, at a show, for example.

# Q

When my pony is in his stable he coughs quite often and he also gives a few harsh dry coughs when I ride him. He eats well and seems perfectly healthy. Is this anything to worry about?

# A

It sounds as though your pony has Chronic Obstructive Pulmonary Disease (COPD). This is an allergic reaction to the spores in stable dust, and often occurs where there is bad ventilation. When the particles enter the lungs, they set up a reaction which obstructs the air flow to the alveoli. So, the lungs cannot work properly.

Once your pony becomes sensitive to dust spores he continues to suffer when he is stabled, unless you lessen the dust levels. Begin by soaking his hay, or feeding a hay substitute (haylage or dried grass), or even feeding a complete cubed ration. Fresh shavings, sawdust, shredded paper, or peat produce less spores than straw, and are better bedding materials for horses with COPD.

# Q

My pony makes a harsh breathing noise when he is cantering. I am concerned that there may be something wrong with his wind.

# A

It sounds as though your pony is 'high blowing'. This is a noise made by vibration within the nasal cavity when he breathes out. It is quite common and is not a sign of disease or injury. It is most often heard in horses with Roman noses, particularly when the head is restrained.

Watch your pony's breath on a cold day. You will probably hear the noise when he breathes *out*, and you have nothing to worry about.

## Q

What is strangles and what symptoms do affected horses show?

## A

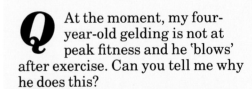

Strangles is a highly infectious disease caused by bacteria called *Streptococcus equi*. Infected horses have a high temperature and look quite poorly. They have a very thick, white discharge and usually cough. The lymph glands beneath the jaw become swollen.

Strangles can be spread directly by coughing, or indirectly by pus or nasal discharge on bedding, tack or the groom's clothing. It is serious and needs immediate veterinary attention because abcesses sometimes form inside the body which can make the pony very ill. Your pony should be isolated until he is better, and until everything has been cleaned and disinfected to prevent the disease from spreading.

Fortunately good immunity develops afterwards so that horses do not get strangles twice.

## Q

When I was grooming my pony the other day I noticed he had a runny nose. Should I be worried?

## A

If the discharge is thick and comes from *one* nostril, it is probably because of a sinus infection. If it is watery and comes from *both* nostrils it is most likely to be caused by a virus infection. If the discharge is *thick* and coming from both nostrils it is usually a sign of bacterial infection.

Keep your pony away from others just in case his condition is catching. Call your vet and ask him or her to examine your pony and diagnose a suitable treatment.

Wiping your pony's nostrils should be part of your daily grooming. As well as keeping the nose clean, it helps you spot any abnormal discharge.

Ponies naturally feed from the ground, which allows mucus and other unwanted material to drain from the nose. If you feed your pony from a wall-mounted manger or hay net this does not happen. Using a portable manger placed on the floor enables discharge to drain as the pony feeds.

## Q

At the moment, my four-year-old gelding is not at peak fitness and he 'blows' after exercise. Can you tell me why he does this?

## A

When a pony is unfit, his muscles need more oxygen to provide energy than they do when he is fit. This need for oxygen goes on for some time after strenuous exercise, such as a gallop, so that heavy breathing and a fast heart rate continue for quite a while after work has finished.

Regular exercise increases the muscles' ability to use oxygen and decreases the need for the horse to 'blow' to provide it. Breathing is a good guide to fitness.

# Eye and ear problems

★ **ADDED EXTRAS**

For extra protection, horses have a third eyelid, which comes across the eye from the inner corner. They also have small, black lumps on their pupils known as *corpora nigra*. These lumps don't appear to have any use and are no cause for worry.

▼ **To keep your pony's** eyes and ears healthy, inspect them regularly.

A horse's sight and hearing are too precious to run any risks with. If you are unsure about an eye or ear condition, call in the vet at once.

## Problem eyes

Because of their prominent position a horse's eyes are prone to injury. Twigs, branches or earth thrown up by the front feet are common causes of trouble.

A horse's response to an eye injury is to keep the eye tightly shut. This produces abnormal amounts of tears, which run down his face and make it difficult to know if the problem is serious. Damage to the retina, for instance, may produce no external signs, but it can be detected by a veterinary surgeon.

Infections in the eye are another risk. Conjunctivitis makes the lining of the eyelids red and sore and can be an indication of more serious trouble.

If there is any sign that a pony's eyesight is not perfect – if he jumps badly or shies regularly – ask your vet to check his eyes. Eye problems grow worse quickly and clear up slowly, so the sooner they are seen to the better.

## Ear trouble

A horse's ears are also prominently placed, but because the delicate hearing mechanisms are well protected inside the head, ear problems are quite rare.

Signs of ear trouble include head shaking, ear rubbing, drooping ear and 'touchy ears', when the horse resents a bridle or headcollar being put on. Blood or watery, pus-like discharge is a sign that something is wrong, as is excessive amounts of brown wax.

Our family pony is 21 years old and we have noticed that the pupil of one of his eyes has developed a white glass-like appearance. Someone suggested he is going blind. Is there anything we can do?

**A**

It sounds as though your pony may have a cataract in one eye. This means that the lens, which should normally be clear, is turning white and preventing the pony seeing properly. If you can see the changes in the lens, the cataract must be quite advanced. Ask your vet to examine the eye to see how the pony's sight is affected. He will check the other eye, just in case the same problem is developing there, too.

Although common in old horses, cataracts don't usually cause any pain. Little can be done to cure them, but luckily horses are good at managing with reduced vision, especially if they are in familiar surroundings. You may be able to carry on riding your pony, but ask your vet whether jumping is safe.

# Q

My pony is always rubbing his ears; could he have mites in his ears and what can I do if he has?

# A

Irritation around the top of the head and upper neck is much more likely to be caused by lice, which are very common in horses during winter and spring. You can clear away lice from a pony's coat using a special de-licing wash or powder. Ask your vet to recommend the most effective brand.

There is one species of mange mite *(Psoroptes equi)*, however, that affects horses. They make the animal shake and rub his ears, and in response the ear produces excessive amounts of brown wax. The vet can check for mites by taking a sample of the wax from your horse's ears. Applying anti-parasite ear drops can quickly help to solve the problem.

▲ ►**Covering** your pony's eyes and ears can prevent him being irritated by flies when he is outside. It also protects these delicate organs from further damage if he is recovering from either an infection, injury or operation.

# Q

My pony's eyes often water. Why is this and what should I do?

# A

A pony's eyes are likely to water when he is at grass and being troubled by flies, or if he has a blocked tear duct. The tears and mucus run down his face and attract yet more flies. It helps to wipe around your pony's eyelids each day with cotton wool or a sponge dampened with clean water. Wipe away any matter sticking to the side of his face, too. If either eye looks red and inflamed, or if the pony is trying to rub them, call in your vet immediately.

# Q

What is conjunctivitis and how do horses get it?

# A

The inner lining of a horse's eyelid, the conjunctiva, is normally a salmon-pink colour. If it is irritated – by dust, hay seeds or flies – it becomes red and swollen and produces discharge. The whole eye feels sore and the horse often makes it worse by rubbing it on his foreleg.

Most cases of conjunctivitis can be cleared up quickly by applying eye drops or ointment containing antibiotics, anti-inflammatory drugs and possibly some local anaesthetic to stop the irritation.

The ointment comes in a tube with a pointed nozzle and must be handled with care to avoid poking the horse in the eye. When applying it, ask someone to hold your pony firmly by the headcollar, so that you have both hands free. Using your thumb and forefinger, pull back the top and bottom lids of the affected eye just enough to reveal the inner edge of the lower lid. Holding the tube horizontally to the eye, run a line of ointment along the lower lid, then release both eyelids. The horse will blink, spreading the ointment across the whole eyeball.

# Allergic reactions

Some horses are sensitive to substances that cause most horses no harm or discomfort. These animals have an allergy. Exposure to the substance causes an allergic reaction and a range of symptoms.

## Cause and effect

The horse's body is protected by his immune system, which fights harmful bacteria and viruses with antibodies. An allergy is an exaggerated reaction of the immune system. The allergen (or the cause of the allergy) could be anything from an insect bite or injection of antibiotics to a feed or mould spores in dusty hay, bedding or concentrates.

When the immune system comes across an allergen it produces antibodies that release chemicals such as histamines – this causes the symptoms of the allergy.

The most common symptom is swelling, usually under the skin and in the lower legs. But an allergic reaction might equally take the form of diarrhoea or a respiratory problem.

**▼ Swelling is one of the most common allergic reactions.** When the body releases chemicals to fight the allergy, fluid is often released into the body tissues, generally under the skin.

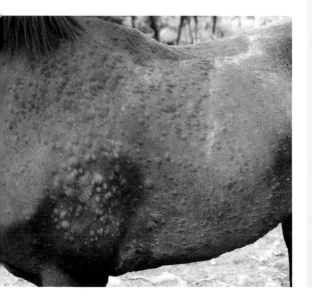

**Q**

When my pony has been out in warm weather, he often develops tiny swellings about 2mm ($\frac{1}{10}$in) in diameter over his back and quarters. They irritate him and make him scratch. Are these swellings an allergic reaction, and, if so, to what?

**A**

No, these are almost certainly just fly or mosquito bites, which are much smaller and more widespread than the swellings produced by an allergic reaction.

An allergic reaction to insect bites causes roundish flat-topped lumps with steep sides. These are about 1-5cm (⅓-2in) in diameter and usually appear on the horse's neck, shoulders, chest, buttocks and abdomen. They cause no itching.

**Q**

A large firm swelling about 2cm (1in) in diameter has recently appeared under my pony's saddle area. It is causing her a great deal of discomfort and pain. Should I burst it?

**A**

No, don't burst it. It could be caused by the larva of the warble fly, which lays its eggs on the surface of the skin. The larva burrows into deeper tissue and resurfaces only when it is ready to hatch. Unless it is removed intact, the larva may release protein and cause a severe allergic reaction that could be fatal if it is not treated rapidly. Consult your vet immediately for advice on removing the lump.

When I work my pony hard, swellings develop on the skin over his back and hindquarters. I have been told that this is an allergy to the high levels of protein in his diet. Is this likely? I changed to a higher protein diet once before without my pony suffering an allergic reaction.

**A**

Yes, it is likely. One of the characteristics of an allergic reaction is that the symptoms never occur the first time the pony comes into contact with the allergen – in this case, increased levels of protein. This makes it difficult to identify the exact cause of the allergy.

Consult an equine nutritionist for advice on the correct balance of protein for the amount of work your pony does. Ponies seldom need a high protein diet – for a tough work schedule, extra carbohydrates are of far more use as they are a valuable source of energy.

**Q**

My pony has developed areas of moist broken skin on his flanks below the saddle area. They are very irritating and make him scratch furiously. Can you tell me what has caused them and how I should treat them?

**A**

Very occasionally, horses develop an allergy to chemicals they come into contact with regularly: dyes or other chemicals in rugs, stable bandages and tack; or biological detergents used to clean numnahs and rugs. When the allergy occurs, it is confined to the area touched by the chemical.

Your pony's broken skin suggests he has an allergy to your rubber riding boots. The only cure is to stop wearing them. Provided you keep the wet areas clean, no treatment should be necessary. If there is a discharge, or the areas look sore, ask your vet for advice.

# The ageing process

Horses change physically and mentally as they get older. Weaker and less hardy than they were when young, they can develop problems that often require special attention.

## Signs of age

There is no definite age when you can say a horse is old. One may be feeling his years at 16, while another may show no signs of age until he is 20.

As he ages, the horse generally slows down. This is because his body systems work less efficiently than in his youth. He may lose weight and become more sensitive to extremes of weather.

Arthritis and rheumatism stiffen an old horse's joints and often cause him pain. His ligaments slacken and have difficulty keeping his legs straight and supporting his spine – he may develop a dipped back, as a result. More than likely, his coat will start to go grey, particularly round the muzzle and eyes.

Although he is generally more able to take things in his stride, the old horse may also become less tolerant of young, boisterous horses – and humans, too.

## A new lifestyle

An old horse needs cosseting. To save him overtiring and straining himself, reduce his work load and, if the vet advises, increase the protein content of his diet to compensate for his less efficient digestive system.

Keep him well sheltered, but don't let him stand without exercise for hours on end – even after a night in the stable an old horse can stiffen up alarmingly. Frequent gentle exercise is best – a daily hack, plus turning out – to keep old joints mobile and reduce stiffness.

The ideal way of keeping an old horse is the combined system, where he is sheltered during bad weather but goes out for exercise and enjoyment. Choose his companions carefully, though – it is best if there are no lively youngsters or bullies round to harass him. If he is miserable while he is out in his field he may lose valuable condition.

Make sure your old horse is warm in winter – use exercise clothing and a New Zealand rug when he's out. In summer, apply a good fly repellent to save him the distress caused by insects.

▼ **An old horse needs special attention** to keep him fit and healthy. He may have to be fed a special diet full of protein to compensate for his less efficient digestive system. Don't be afraid to pamper your old horse with tasty treats – he deserves them!

## Q

My old pony has recently started dipping his back and moving away when I try to saddle him up. Why is this and what should I do?

## A

His back conformation may have changed as he's grown older, so that his saddle no longer fits. If his saddle hurts him, he will associate tacking up with the pain of being ridden and try to avoid it. Ask an expert to check the saddle's fit and have a saddler adjust it if necessary. Although it is no substitute for a correctly fitting saddle, a thick numnah may ease the pain. If the pain continues, call a vet as your pony could have a back injury that needs to be investigated.

## Q

Often when I bring my elderly pony out first thing in the morning, he doesn't really want to walk – sometimes he even has difficulty getting up. After we've been out for a while, he loosens up. What's wrong with him?

## A

Your pony could be suffering from arthritis, which causes his joints to stiffen and can be extremely painful. Call the vet, who will be able to confirm what's wrong with your pony and prescribe medicines to ease the discomfort – your pony may need to take these medicines for the rest of his life.

An arthritic pony needs to be kept warm and dry. Make sure that he is rugged up before being turned out in cold or rainy weather and provide a shelter for him in the field. Your old pony should have frequent gentle exercise, but make sure you have really warmed him up by walking and trotting before doing anything more strenuous, such as cantering.

## Q

When I turn my old horse out he often stands by the gate and, after a short while, asks to come in again. This happens most in wet or windy weather or when the sun is hot and there are lots of flies. Is he ill?

## A

No, he's simply undergoing the normal ageing process. Older animals are often less able to cope with extremes of weather. Provide him with a field shelter so that he can escape the weather and flies. Alternatively, turn him out in summer in the cool of the evening and bring him in during the day. In winter, put a New Zealand rug on him before you turn him out.

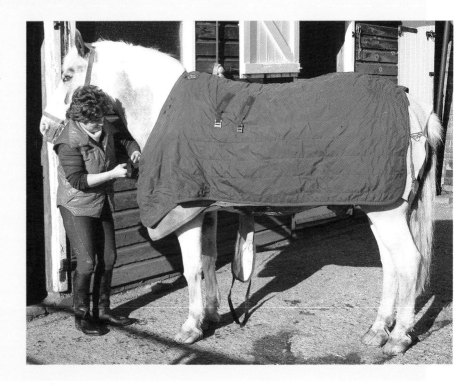

# INDEX

NEWTON LE WILLOWS
LIBRARY
TEL.01744 677885/86/87

# PICTURE ACKNOWLEDGMENTS

*Photographs:* Page 1 NHPA/Henry Ausloos, 2-3 Kit Houghton, 4-5 Woodfall Wild Images/David Woodfall, 6-7 (Chapter One) Ardea London Ltd/Liz Bomford, 38-39 (Chapter Two) Animal Photography/Sally-Anne Thompson, 64-65 (Chapter Three) Bob Langrish, (Chapter Four) Animal Photography/Sally-Anne Thompson, (Chapter Five) Bob Langrish.

9(l) Oxford Scientific Films/Bomford & Borkowski, (r) FLPA/Terry Whittaker, 10 Bob Langrish, 11(t) J.Allan Cash, (c) Animal Photography/Sally-Ann Thompson, (bl) Shona Wood, (br) Bob Langrish, 12(t) NHPA/Agence Nature, (b) Getty Images, 13(l) Animal Photography/Sally-Ann Thompson, (r) AGE Fotostock, 18 EM/Shona Wood, 19(tl,c,b) EM/Shona Wood, (tr) Bruce Coleman/Jane Burton, 22 Martin E. Dalby, 24(t) Kit Houghton, (b) EM/Shona Wood, 25-27 EM/Shona Wood, 28 Getty Images, 29(t) AGE Fotostock, (c) Animal Photography/R.Willbie, (b) Bob Langrish, 30 The Stock Market, 31(t,b) Kit Houghton, (c) Aquila/Robert Maier, 32(t) Elisabeth Weiland, (b) EM/Shona Wood, 33(t) EM/Shona Wood, (b) Getty Images, 34 Getty Images, 35(t) Animal Photography/Sally-Ann Thompson, (c) Bob Langrish, (b) Aquila/Robert Maier, 36, 37(t,c) EM/Shona Wood, 37(b) Bob Langrish, 41, 43 Kit Houghton, 44(t) Robert Estall, (b) EM/Shona Wood, 45(t,c) EM/Shona Wood, (b) The Slide File, 46 Mike Roberts/Only Horses, 47(t) EM/Shona Wood, (b) Mike Roberts/Only Horses, 48-49 Kit Houghton, 50-51 EM/Shona Wood, 52(t) EM/Shona Wood, (b) Oxford Scientific Films/Liz and Tony Bomford, 53(t) Bob Langrish, (b) EM/John Suett, 54 EM/Shona Wood, 55(tl) Bob Langrish, (r) EM/Elisabeth Weiland, (b) Elisabeth Weiland, 56(t) Nature Photographers/S.C.Bisserot, 56-7(b) NHPA/Stephen Dalton, 57(t) EM/Elisabeth Weiland, (br) Neil Holmes, 58(t) Animal Photography/R.Willbie, (b) Aquila/Robert Maier, 59(t) Bob Langrish, (b) The Stock Market, 60 Kit Houghton, 61(tl) Bob Langrish, (tr) EM/Shona Wood, (b) Bob Langrish, 62-63 EM/Shona

Wood, 63(t) Bob Langrish, 66(t) Bruce Coleman/Hans Reinhard, (b) Elisabeth Weiland, 67 Elisabeth Weiland, 68-69 EM/Shona Wood, 70(t) EM/Shona Wood, (b) Martin E. Dalby, 71 Kit Houghton, 72-73 EM/Shona Wood, 74 EM/Shona Wood, 75 Bruce Coleman Ltd, 76-77 The Stock Market, 77(t) Aquila/Robert Maier, (c) Robert Estall/Octopus Books, (b) Bruce Coleman/Hans Reinhard, 82 Elisabeth Weiland, 83 Kit Houghton, 84-85 Bob Langrish, 86(t) Kit Houghton, (b) Aquila/Robert Maier, 87(t) Bob Langrish, (b) Martin E. Dalby, 88 Martin E. Dalby, 89(t) Aquila/Robert Maier, (b) Bob Langrish, 90-91 Aquila/Robert Maier, 92-93 EM/Shona Wood, 94(t) Bob Langrish, (b) EM/Shona Wood, 95 EM/Shona Wood, 96-97 EM/Karen Clark, 98 Aquila/Robert Maier, (inset) EM/Shona Wood, 99(t) EM/Shona Wood, (b) Oxford Scientific Films/Jeff Foott, 100 Kit Houghton, 101(t) EM/Elisabeth Weiland, (c) EM/Shona Wood, (b) Martin E. Dalby, 102-103 Aquila/Robert Maier, 104-105 EM/Shona Wood, 105 Elisabeth Weiland, 106 Aquila/Robert Maier, 107(t) Elisabeth Weiland, (b) Bruce Coleman/Hans Reinhard, 108 EM/Shona Wood, 109(t) EM/Shona Wood, (b) Aquila/Robert Maier, 110(t) Oxford Scientific Films/Jeff Foott, 110-111(b) EM/Shona Wood, 111(t) Oxford Scientific Films/Jeff Foott, 112-113 EM/Shona Wood, 114-115 Aquila/Robert Maier, 116 NHPA/Peter Johnson, 117(t) Bruce Coleman, (b) Kit Houghton, 118-119 Animal Photography/Sally-Ann Thompson, 120-122 EM/Shona Wood, 123(t) EM/Shona Wood, (b) Bob Langrish, 124-5 Getty Images, 126-127 Martin E. Dalby, 128(t) Martin E. Dalby, (bl) Kit Houghton, (br) Bob Langrish, 129 Bruce Coleman/Hans Reinhard, 132(t) EM/Shona Wood, (b) Bob Langrish, 133(t) EM/Shona Wood, (b) Martin E. Dalby, 134-135 Bruce Coleman/Jonathan Wright, 135(t) Bob Langrish, (b) EM/Shona Wood, 136-137 Getty Images, 137(t) Bruce Coleman/Fritz Prenzel, (b) Elisabeth Weiland, 138 Martin E. Dalby, 139(t) EM/Martin E. Dalby, (b) EM/Shona Wood, 140 Aquila, 141(tr) EM/Shona Wood, (b) EM/Nick Rains, 142-143 Animal

Photography/Sally-Ann Thompson, 144-145 Aquila/Robert Maier, 146(t) EM/Shona Wood, (b) Bruce Coleman/Jeff Foott, 147 Bob Langrish, 148-155 EM/Shona Wood, 156-157 Nature Photographers/Roger Tidman, 158(t) EM/Shona Wood, (bl) Peter Roberts, (br) EM/Shona Wood, 159-161 EM/Shona Wood, 162 (main) EM/Shona Wood, (inset) Kit Houghton, 163(t,bl) Bob Langrish, (c,br) Kit Houghton, 164 Kit Houghton, 165,166 EM/Shona Wood, 167(tr) Kit Houghton, (b) Bob Langrish, 168-173 EM/Shona Wood, 174(t) EM/Shona Wood, 174-175(b) Kit Houghton, 175(t) EM/Shona Wood, (b) Martin E. Dalby, 178(t) Kit Houghton, (b) EM/Shona Wood, 179-182 EM/Shona Wood, 183(t) Kit Houghton, (b) EM/Shona Wood, 184-187 EM/Shona Wood, 187(r) Bob Langrish, 188-189 EM/Shona Wood, 190(t,br) Bob Langrish, (c) Robert Harding Picture Library, (bl) EM/Shona Wood, 191 Bob Langrish, 192-193 EM/Shona Wood, 194-195 Kit Houghton, 195(t) Animal Photography/Sally-Ann Thompson, 197 Martin E. Dalby, 198(t) EM/Shona Wood, (b) Bob Langrish, 199 EM/Shona Wood, 200 EM/Shona Wood, 201 Gillian McCarthy/Equine Management Consultancy Service, (c) EM/Shona Wood, (b) Bob Langrish, 202(t) Kit Houghton, (b) Rod Fisher, 203 EM/Shona Wood, 204 Jacana, 205 EM/Shona Wood.

*Illustrations:* 8-9 Catherine Constable, 14-15, 20-21 Joan Thompson/Garden Studios, 23(t) Catherine Constable, (b) Joan Thompson/Garden Studios, 40 Catherine Constable, 41 Denys Ovenden, 42-43 Catherine Constable, 44-45, 50-51, 78-79 Maggie Rayner, 80-81 Joan Thompson/Garden Studios, 127 Denys Ovenden, 137 Maggie Rayner, 159 Denys Ovenden.

EM=Eaglemoss Publications Ltd, FLPA=Frank Lane Picture Agency, NHPA=Natural History Picture Agency.